YOU COULD FEEL GOOD

by
Suzanne Harrill

Copyright © 1987 by Suzanne Harrill

All rights reserved. No part of this work may be reproduced or transmitted in any form or by any means, electronic or mechanical, including photocopying and recording, or by any information storage and retrieval system, except as may be expressly permitted by the 1976 Copyright Act or in writing by the publisher.

Request for such permission should be addressed to:

> Uni★Sun
> P.O. Box 25421
> Kansas City, MO 64119

This book is manufactured in the United States of America. Cover art by Bradley Dehner and distribution by The Talman Company.

> The Talman Company, Inc.
> 150 Fifth Avenue
> New York, N.Y. 10011

ISBN # 0-912949-17-1
LCCN: 87-051684

A Uni★Sun BOOK

Table of Contents

Introduction ix

Part I: Feeling Good

Chapter 1—Breaking Out of Old Patterns:
        The Steps of Change 1
Chapter 2—Self-Esteem: The Foundation 13
Chapter 3—Concepts That Build Self-Esteem 21
Chapter 4—True and False Guiding Beliefs 35
Chapter 5—Tools for Change 59
Chapter 6—The Author's Process of Writing This Book.... 69

Part II: Workbook for Feeling Good

Section 1—The Self-Esteem Indicator 81
Section 2—Affirmations 85
Section 3—Visualizations 93
Section 4—Thoughts to Ponder 97
Section 5—Further Suggestions 99
Section 6—Self-Awareness Exercises 103
Section 7—Suggested Readings 105

Appendix: Five People Share Their Experiences 107
Poem by A Friend 117
Conclusion: A Final Thought 119

Notes and Acknowledgments

Dedication

This book is dedicated to several of my teachers: Ann Alexander, L. S. Barksdale, Bert Boquet, Cindy Jackson, Ken Keyes, Paul Solomon, and Patricia Sun.

Thank You

Thank you to all my clients and students who have shared and allowed me to learn from you. Thank you to Anita, Chris, Diane, Dorothy, Jerry, Jo, Kim, Margo, Nanci, Sue and Victoria.

A Special Acknowledgment

I especially acknowledge Rodney, my husband, who is also my teacher. Rodney, more than anyone, has helped me to know that the concepts in this book are livable and valid in everyday life! I also acknowledge my three daughters—Lindy, Janna, and Sarah.

Notation

The names of people in this book have been changed to keep my clients anonymous.

Permission

Quotations from this book may be used without restriction for the purpose of helping others. Please give credit to the author.

Sound self-esteem is the feeling of
total acceptance and love for yourself
as you are
regardless of what you may now see
as your faults, problems, or mistakes
regardless of your looks, weight, race, or IQ.

Self-esteem is a quiet, comfortable place
of enjoying being who you are.
It is knowing who you *really* are:
your Self.

When you live being who you are
you Feel Good.

Introduction

The creation of a thousand forests is in one acorn.
—Ralph Waldo Emerson

This book is about change and feeling good. It tells how to feel good about yourself just the way you are. Many people do not believe it is possible to feel good, but I've learned it is possible. My job is teaching this to others. Everything I will be telling you is based on personal experience. It is what has worked for me, and I'd like to share it with you.

I am not describing an imaginary, idealistic state of being. I have truly changed my life, as you can, too. I used to have a good day if my husband had a good day and a bad day if he had a bad day. Now I have good days and occasional off days (I don't like the word "bad"), depending on my own real feelings; but *my* feelings are no longer determined by other people's feelings and moods of the moment (even if I sometimes forget, temporarily).

Let me illustrate one circumstance that used to make me feel bad. At one time I over-identified with my oldest daughter, Lindy, when she had what I considered to be too much homework in the fourth grade. She was not organized at that time in her life (and I have learned many fourth graders are not), and Lindy would come home from school and forget exactly what her assignments were. She would scream and cry when I tried to organize her schedule so that she could get it all done by a certain time. It seemed that there was never enough time to do all the homework and little time for play and fun.

I felt overly responsible for her, and she learned quickly to let me take that responsibility. It was a tough year for both of us, and no sooner would we see each other after school than a heavy cloud hung over us both with little joy. We dreaded the evening that lay ahead if it was a heavy homework night. I found myself feeling happy if there was little or no homework and unhappy if there was a lot of homework.

While I was involved in this drama, I did not see my part in it; nor did I see that I had any choices. I did have choices, of course, but I was unwilling at that point in time to allow her to fail or to do poorly. If she did poorly, I would feel that I had failed, whereas with more awareness I could have seen that she needed to take responsibility for her own choices. I could have chosen to communicate to her how I felt and the values I wanted for her, and could have listened more deeply to her responses. (If I *had* to *do* something, I could better have used my energy in exercising vigorously or just going for a pleasant walk, for my own benefit!) But my rigid guiding beliefs about what a good mother did included the idea that I had to teach my child responsibility, and responsibility to me meant doing everything that was ever asked of me without questioning whether it was a realistic expectation.

This experience was one crisis that forced me to gather information and learn new patterns of behavior. Today, when one of my daughters gets in this situation, I am able to turn loose of whether all the homework is done, done correctly, or done by a certain time. I get involved to help and encourage if needed. Occasionally I'll even catch myself beginning to feel bad if the evening is not going smoothly; then I realize that there are better choices of ways to handle the situation.

This incident illustrates something about patterns that we live out that are unhealthy and keep us stuck, feeling bad. While writing this book I have opened myself to consciously seeing in depth one of the patterns that influenced me from my family of origin. For example, this drama about homework opened up new information and also some very helpful communication. When my mother read the manuscript for this book, she shared with me some decisions she had made about homework when I was very young. After watching a close friend of hers get very involved with her child, doing homework for hours every evening, my mother decided she would not get involved in that way with me. Her decision illustrates one reaction to things we do not like in life, which is to go to the opposite extreme.

My mother's decision to avoid getting involved with much homework later influenced me when I made the opposite decision to help every day with my child's homework. These were flip sides of the same pattern. The difficulties I recalled about doing my own homework well also influenced this decision. I had felt great frustration over not having the planning skills needed to handle my homework load and the thinking skills needed to get high grades. When my daughter showed similar frustrations, I wanted to protect her from the same pain I had felt. I now see I was overstepping my boundaries—my daughter was not me. A good balance would be somewhere between these two extremes.

Looking back now, I do not judge these experiences over homework as good or bad, right or wrong. I am simply aware of a pattern in my family, and I am healing my own interpretation of what made me unhappy and frustrated for years. I can let go of earlier resentment at not being supported to get high grades through help from my parents. In fact, that aspect of our adventure together was later strengthening because it made me determine within myself to gain my goals on my own.

It was humbling to realize that I had made the same "mistake" with my own child! I failed to understand her feelings about her homework assignments because I over-reacted to the memory of my own childhood feelings. Of course, when I realized that I was helping too much, I stopped; and she is now finding her own inner strength to meet her own needs as she sees them. And so am I. Maybe this is the scheme by which life teaches its real lessons, and love is the atmosphere that finally makes it a positive experience.

Let me back track a little and share with you how I gathered much of the factual information in this book. In the late 1970's my husband, Rodney, was transferred to the small town of Thibodaux, Louisiana. Though not thrilled about the move at first, I gained enthusiasm when I learned that there was a small university in the town, and I began imagining (a technique you will learn for creating) myself teaching there. The day after I arrived, I telephoned Nicholls State University and located a group called Special Services. It was here that I had the good fortune to meet and work with many loving and giving people. One of them was Ralph Morel, a man I worked for; he encouraged me and gave me many of the teaching materials that he had gathered. Whenever I went to his office, I always came back with enough handouts to use for the next ten years. One day I asked, "Ralph, why do you give me so many materials that are yours?"

He replied, "Because I know you'll pass them on." What a role model for me to emulate! And whenever I can, I do pass them on.

Another gift I received was a book titled *Building Self-Esteem* by the late L. S. Barksdale; it was part of the course I taught called Student Development. Barksdale's book opened many doors for me, and I have taught many classes based upon it. This book was the catalyst for me to teach and eventually to learn, from personal experience and from working with others, that people can learn to feel good about themselves. His ideas have greatly influenced this book.

INTRODUCTION

Why change? Why feel good?

Feeling good feels good! It makes life a beautiful and worthwhile experience. It puts you in a healthy state of mind so that you can change what needs to be changed in your life and can accept what you cannot change and need to accept.

Feeling good is feeling empowered. Feeling good is feeling worthy. Feeling good enables you to take responsibility for bringing good things into your own life. If you feel good, you face situations with confidence; and regardless of what may happen to you or to others, you can handle each new day as it comes. You begin to see that life's challenges are not a series of threats but are exciting opportunities for growth. Finally, feeling good is experiencing inner peace which radiates from you more and more as it becomes your way of life.

I can hear some of you saying now, "Yes, but she doesn't know anything about *my* kind of stress—my conflicts, my problems, my children, my job." But I do know. I have dealt with many stressful issues in my life. Painful conflict was the catalyst that first made me seek answers to what I saw as major problems.

I have had many challenges on my journey to feeling good. I learned to balance my needs against other people's needs and to let go of guilt when I choose to put myself and my needs first at times. I've balanced career needs and family needs. I've certainly learned patience with three daughters, a husband, and two dogs, to name just a few of my responsibilities. I've learned about commitment, communication, trust, anger, fear, and turning over my power in a primary love relationship. I could go on, but you can see what I mean. I do know what it is like not to feel good, to have low self-esteem, to feel stuck in problems, and to feel pain.

I have also been very close to many other people who have shared their pain in areas that I have not experienced: death, divorce, physical illness, physical handicap, alcoholism, poverty and early childhood abuse. I have seen the ideas in this book work for all types of problems and pain. In reality there are no distinctions as to who has a greater problem. Pain is pain whether it be physical, emotional, mental, or spiritual.

A very significant improvement in my self-esteem came about when I stopped feeling victimized by others. This change began with a startling statement by one of my graduate school instructors: "No one can hurt you without your own permission."

Initially I doubted this assertion. My feelings in those days were hurt easily and often. Rejection was my favorite fear. I felt that others were insensitive, or even intentionally hurtful; and I found myself questioning and pondering what this teacher could possibly mean by her strange statement.

As a child I had often felt bad about myself if my mother emotionally distanced herself from me. Like any parent, she sometimes did not like my behavior. Other times she was in a bad mood not related to me. When she happened to be angry, I just assumed I had done something to cause the anger. A lump would come in my stomach, I would feel nauseated when she was angry or upset, and I would try to find ways to make her emotionally close to me again in order to restore my own emotional security. This extreme reaction is what family therapists call enmeshment. Emotionally, I did not have my own boundaries and I attracted to myself anything that significant others in my life were feeling. If they were in emotional pain, I was too. I seemed unable to control my own mental and emotional space if my mother was not behaving or feeling as I wanted her to.

My insecurities and lack of boundaries carried right over to my relationship with my husband when I got married. I am now very grateful that he was strong enough to act out the drama with me and to help in changing these unwholesome patterns. Fortunately (I can say now) Rodney had some of the traits that my mother had, so it was very easy for me to transfer familiar anxieties to him. We had ample opportunities to act out and to clarify the old patterns, and our effort in doing this helped me heal some unhealthy aspects in all my close relationships.

One pattern that has been greatly healed is the disruption and feelings of helplessness I had when Rodney was in a bad mood. I was unable in the early years of our marriage to function well if Rodney was withdrawn, uncommunicative and short tempered. I would cry—alone—and be very quiet and submissive. I felt like I had done something "wrong" and therefore had better "be good." This meant figuring out "intuitively" what he wanted and doing it, even if it was not fair to me, in order to be loved and touched. It could be as small an issue as fixing left-overs for dinner and he would eat only a very small portion. In those days, Rodney could not express his needs and say, "I really do not like chili—when this pot is gone, let's not have it for a couple of years." Instead, he would express dislike by eating in silence, eating only a half bowl, and finally saying, "Why did you fix chili again?"

In those days I could not separate my cooking from who I was. I felt he did not like me when he criticized my cooking. I could not tell that he was worried about a homework assignment (we married in college) or had other things "off" in his day which were not related to me. The only way I was able to handle the feelings was to cry. I felt awful, hurt, and lonely. I was not able to express feelings; in fact, I didn't even know what they were.

After many years of studying and reading, I began to understand the dynamics of our relationship. I have only one regret at this time—that I did not seek counseling. I would not have been in pain for so long if I had asked for help. I can see now that I was not even focused on needing help. All I lived for were the perfect moments when Rodney and I were in sync. That was when I was "happy." Emotionally, I was on a real roller coaster.

Much of the information in this book is what I figured out on my own, or with help from teachers (the support that started showing up when I was 30 years old).

Two experiences that helped us greatly were a Marriage Encounter weekend (sponsored by various churches) and a family therapy course in graduate school. In the Marriage Encounter weekend, Rodney and I learned what feelings were and how to write and talk about them with each other. For the first time, we learned not to judge, criticize, or try to change our partner. We learned to play the game of life on the same team. The family therapy course opened a whole new world of viewing myself. It taught me about family dramas, secrets and patterns that affect us. It made me see what healthy and unhealthy family dynamics were. One of the simplest things that changed my feelings of rejection was learning to communicate and share directly with Rodney, letting him know what his effect on me was, and not being afraid to find out what was really bothering him.

I can still sometimes fall into my old patterns of trying to please others in order not to feel rejected. However, I am not stuck there. I soon regain my perspective and am comfortable in taking responsibility for myself and acting from my own motives. Similarly, I respect the right of others to claim their own self-determination, and do not fall into the trap of a power struggle. Allowing family, friends, or clients to have their experiences (even when it is not to my liking) is a part of choosing to be powerful rather than victimized in dealing with my own experiences.

I have found that one overriding concept is necessary to a healthy sense of self-worth. It is the knowledge that you are perfect, right now, just the way you are. This thought is best illustrated by looking at an acorn. The acorn (which has become my symbol of the beauty and perfection that you are, regardless of your problems, early childhood, body, I.Q., mistakes, etc.) is a perfect expression of its Self at every phase of its growing. It is no less worthy as a seed with all its potential hidden from view than as a full grown tree. All along the acorn's life path (as a seedling, a small tree, a big tree, and a giant tree) it is perfect; it is being who and what it is capable of being at every moment. Even though it is capable of growing more at each stage of its life, the acorn is still a beautiful expression of its Self at every stage. And you, like the acorn, are a beautiful expression of your Self. It is necessary to allow this idea of present perfection to be a part of your belief system in order to truly feel good about yourself now. Feeling good involves a process of removing blockages and allowing the full expression of your Self to be felt.

As you read these pages, you will learn again what you once knew innately. You are worthy simply because you exist. I hope that as you read, you will recall your own original awareness that this is true.

There are two parts to this book. Part One gives you an understanding of what feeling good is about.

Chapter One begins with the steps people go through when they begin growing, changing, and transforming. Knowing these steps helps us to be less fearful of change and to stop resisting the growth process.

Chapter Two presents the fundamentals of feeling good: building sound self-esteem. This is the firm foundation needed to feel good about yourself.

Chapter Three continues with self-esteem concepts such as accepting yourself right now, the way you are, and not judging yourself with "shoulds" and "oughts." You will learn to separate the essence of who you are from your behavior.

Chapter Four deals with things you *were taught* that are *not true* and with things that *are true* that you were *not taught*. This chapter explains how your guiding beliefs affect what you experience in life. Whatever you *believe* is true for *you;* even if it is not a universal truth, you will operate your life as if it were the truth.

Chapter Five gives two techniques that can change your life: affirmations and visualizations. By reprogramming your self-talk and the pictures in your mind, you can create consciously what you want in your life.

Finally, Chapter Six is the description of my personal experience in writing this book.

Part Two is a workbook to help make Part One practical and useful through exercises which will help you incorporate these principles in your own life.

The Appendix includes letters from five people I've worked with who are willing to share with you some of the ways the information has helped them.

You may want to take my Self-Esteem Indicator in Section One on Page 81 at this time, and to take it again from time to time as you grow.

I wish you well on your journey.

Love,

Suzanne

Part I

Feeling Good

Chapter One

Breaking Out of Old Patterns: The Steps of Change

> Learning about yourself—your feelings, your belief systems, your deepest fears, and your most intense emotions—will be a process you will never want to end once you have experienced its rewards.
>
> —Jeanne Segal, *Living Beyond Fear*

Why did you select this book to read? Was it because you are ready to change your life, to break out of old patterns, and to create new ones? Was it because you are in crisis, or because you are tired of being bored, ill, or unhappy? Maybe you once left a relationship or job feeling victimized and then, further down the path of life, you entered a new relationship or job and again felt victimized. If the people and events change in your life but the problems stay the same, you may be caught in old, unneeded patterns. If this happens to you, it is you who needs to change.

There are several steps in the process of breaking free from old patterns. Knowing these steps helps you to understand and accept your unfamiliar feelings and emotions. The first step in the transformational process is having something happen to you that catches your attention. It can be a life shock such as a divorce, an accident, or an illness. It can be a state of confusion associated with what is called a "nervous breakdown." Your normal boundaries of acceptable behavior and the ability to focus your attention may be replaced with anxiety, crying, inability to concentrate, or depression. Actually, you need this confusion and loss of control. These symptoms can call attention to your own unhealthy thought patterns which are not otherwise conscious to you but which are keeping you in bondage to a limited lifestyle—a lifestyle that you are now ready to discard.

So you are ready to look for ways out of your situation. During the second step you read books, get counseling, or take classes. You look into building self-esteem, improving relationships, or learning effective communication; maybe you take assertiveness training. This is your information-gathering step. An elevated state of awareness is often experienced in the beginning of step two. You seem to know how you got to where you are, and you seem to have a clear idea of where you are going. A certain optimism is present, and this optimism helps you initially to escape from some of your earlier inhibitions.

The third step is becoming aware that you have been blindly stuck and repeating a pattern. Before this realization you often felt sorry for yourself; you saw yourself as victimized by others. But now you are ready to take charge of your life, to establish new patterns, and to express who you really are. It's okay if your progress at first feels a little "iffy." One day you may handle your life well, and the next day you may fall back into old patterns. It is likely you'll sometimes feel depressed at being unable to put into practice the new information you have gained. Some days the old tapes in your mind will almost convince you, "I can't be different—I've got to do whatever (name) expects—I wonder what made me think I could change THAT!" But it is too late to turn back. Even if you do feel discouraged, you now also feel a sense of responsibility for your own destiny that you did not feel earlier. And your desire to get out of the old rut is beginning to outweigh your fear of giving up the familiar. You feel pulled in opposite directions; it is a feeling of being in no-man's land.

Now you are ready for the difficult fourth step: taking real risks. This period involves a stormy, uncomfortable battle between all your feelings on the inside and your relationships on the outside. In step three you experimented with small, calculated risks. But now you are beginning to speak, act, and react differently to people and events. Doing so brings both release and chaos. A part of you is joyful because you are consciously choosing to encounter life on your own terms. You are acting out new and healthy patterns, and you "collide" frequently with your old patterns. Breaking out of them brings relief, and it also may bring pain. The reaction of others is not always supportive, although sometimes it is. Those who found your previous demeanor convenient will be puzzled. If you love such a person but reject the level of control he/she has had over your life, you must find new ways to express love and support while continuing to establish your new patterns of self-determination. Step four is not easy, but part of you can now say, "At last! I'm nearing my own liberation!"

The final step can be summed up in one word: acceptance. Accept that you have broken out of your old patterns and belief systems. You now see your early programming objectively. You do not have to keep fighting it all your life; you have earned the right to leave it behind. You see that your early programming did serve a purpose in its time. It helped you to blend into the family, the clan, and the culture into which you were born. As a child you received your patterns of behavior from authority figures outside yourself, and you conformed your life to others' expectations. But now you have internalized the pattern givers. By going through steps one through four described above, you have thrown off unnecessary limitations, discarded the patterns that once inhibited your adult expression, and finally claimed responsibility for directing your own life.

You are now free to be grateful for both the guidance and the difficult learning experiences of your childhood years. You can forgive your own reluctance to take charge of your own life, and you are securely your own person. I might add here that you never reach a place without challenge and growth. What is different is that you begin to love and support yourself whenever you are going through a difficult passage. Rather than be a victim of the pain, you interpret differently what you see and feel in the course of your experience. For example, I may briefly feel insecure if someone disagrees with me; but my secure base of loving myself allows me to realize quickly that this apparent drama is rooted in an old interpretation of a similar event, and I, thus, release any helpless feeling that may surface and can respond objectively in the moment. The challenge is not in meeting occasional disagreement; it is in being able to accept wholesomely the person who disagrees.

Let me illustrate these steps with Angela, who recently left her marriage. The first three years that she was married, all seemed well. Then one day she woke up depressed and crying without really knowing why; she was aware that she had resisted crying for a long time. She had stopped communicating her frustrations and fears to her husband after the infatuation of being married died. Since Tim, her husband, no longer asked about her frustrations or drew her out as he had in the beginning of their relationship, Angela had bottled up a lot of feelings. When she began crying, she could not seem to stop, although she did learn to control her emotions long enough to go to work and come home. In a classic step one reaction, Angela's problems were being brought to her attention.

Finally Angela asked for help, and this is when she entered step two. She began therapy and began taking self-awareness classes. She loved it at first because she had an immediate sense of relief. The more she learned, the more she realized how unhealthy some of her patterns of communication were and how inadequate she felt in expressing herself. The new information helped, and she began to realize there was much that needed to be changed.

Now Angela was in step three, which was a kind of "no man's land" for her. The need for change was often obvious, and yet intense fear came up while making the changes. For Angela one fear in particular, rejection, crippled her when she began to assert her needs and feelings to her husband. Because he was frightened by her direct behavior, he withdrew and would not respond to her. Angela was unable to see his pain and became inhibited by his withdrawal. She would stop being assertive and would become nauseated. Fear of his rejection made her revert to her old, submissive, "giving" patterns; however these compliant behaviors would then cause her to feel depressed. She couldn't feel good in doing either the old or the new behavior. The conflict between the security of familiar patterns and the freedom and growth of establishing new patterns became conscious for Angela.

Because Angela participated in a support group and continued to gain insight in therapy, she eventually moved through this double bind and did make a positive change. Her frustration with old, unhealthy patterns of poor communication with her husband finally triggered a willingness to risk any consequences that might result from taking direct action.

This readiness to take a risk was step four in the process of Angela's change; the culmination of step four was a divorce: the only solution since Tim would not involve himself in her process of growth. He could not see Angela's need for broader horizons; perhaps he liked the convenience of her submissiveness. In any case he refused to help heal the pain and create a healthy relationship.

Angela is now out of the relationship and is in step five. She accepts her own decision to choose positive self-growth over an unwholesome marriage. A year has passed, and she has met someone who is also pursuing self-growth and who has grown through therapy as Angela has. She still recalls the time during the grieving process following the divorce when she felt like going back to the marriage for "security." Had she done so, she could have fallen right back into the old patterns which she had actually outgrown; however with support she gained increased confidence in her own self-worth and continued growing in self-determination.

This illustration is an extreme example. One does not always have to experience such consequences. Jane went through a similar growth process and found that her husband was ready for new growth in the marriage. They have created a rewarding and fulfilling relationship by choosing to make changes together.

When Jane was in pain, so was her husband, Bob. When she had the courage to begin therapy, she would share her process with Bob. He at first just listened and was relieved that Jane was getting help. Eventually he entered therapy with her. At first he was participating to please her; but after awhile, learned much about himself. He chose to become active in the process of therapy, choosing self-awareness and improving his communication skills as well.

Looking back on my own life, I could apply these very steps to the years from 30 to 38. My inner world began to fall apart. I was unhappy with just about every aspect of my life. I felt depressed. I did not like the things I talked about with old friends, nor did I like my relationship with my husband and my kids. I cried, I complained. I wanted to leave. By noticing that some of my life patterns did not serve me any more, I had entered step one,

Pain is telling you that:

*Something is "wrong."

*Something is "off."

*Something needs changing.

*Something is coming into your Awareness.

though actually the crisis had been building for many years.

In step two I read books, took classes, and sought counseling. I became more aware of how little I knew about myself, my needs, my fears, my lacks, my purpose, and my potentials. I had achieved what I earlier had set out in life to achieve, and life was no longer satisfying. I needed a greater sense of purpose. I wanted to know what I could do to improve my personality imbalances. In my relationships with my husband, children, friends and family of origin, I wanted understanding, acceptance, love, and joy. As if this were not enough, I wanted a different relationship with God. I wanted to really know what life was about and how I fit into the greater whole.

During step three, I spent about seven years gathering information, looking at possibilities for myself and changing my awareness. I read many books and met many very interesting people who each gave me pieces to the puzzle of putting myself together.

Ponder on This, by Alice Bailey, was one of the books that changed my life. I do not recommend it for many people, however, because it is very hard to read; its meaning is heavily veiled or hidden. This book explains the spiritual journey we humans are in. I had been searching for answers to what the universe was about and here were many answers. From there I read such books as *The Nature of Personal Reality,* by Jane Roberts; *Grist for the Mill,* by Ram Dass; *The Handbook to Higher Consciousness,* by Ken Keyes; and *A Course in Miracles.* There were dozens more. All of these books began merging to knit a fabric upon which to lay the patterns of my being. One teacher I found was Elliott Goldwag, who edited the book, *Inner Balance.* The class he taught was about a holistic approach to health and to life. I learned from him about *A Course in Miracles,* a book transcribed by a Jewish woman who was a traditional psychotherapist. This woman does not believe she wrote the book; therefore she does not put her name on it. She would wake up at night and transcribe the words of the book as they came into her mind. She had not been aware of many of the concepts prior to that time. The *Course* written in this way is about such things as healing, miracles, forgiveness, and Christ Consciousness.

At the same time, I met a personal teacher who answered hundreds of questions for me. He helped me understand much of what I had been reading as well as understand myself and the members of my family.

At one point in this period, I even took voice lessons from a delightful woman. My goal was self-awareness, self-expression, and self-confidence—not to become a singer. She helped me to understand more about myself and how I held back on my power. The breathing exercises for singing greatly improved my physical stamina.

As if all this were not enough, I began to meditate during this period; and I began to write. I kept learning more and more about a greater me. All these new developments illustrate a very intense step three.

Then I entered step four. It was time now to act on the information I had gathered. For one thing, I became aware of my needs to work for myself and to teach classes on building self-esteem. This realization was great for my personal growth; however, it presented me with some unexpected challenges. It brought up some old patterns of living that would have to go. As life would have it, only my night classes filled up. This was in direct opposition to the lifestyle I had created up to that time! In the past I had always been home every evening and been available to my husband and three children. I needed to do what was right for me. In order to change that pattern, I had to face what I interpreted as disapproval at home. It was a tremendous emotional strain on me (and everyone else) to do what was right for me: to self-actualize, to use my talents in order to feel good about myself, and to let go of my old pattern of doing only what others gave me permission to do. I had the opportunity to confront my fears about rejection, my anger for turning my power over to others, and my feelings of guilt for not pleasing my loved ones.

I finally made it through that passage. It took about three years. I now accept the new patterns and lifestyle that I have created for myself, and I now have the support, acceptance, and encouragement of my family. The process has been worth it!

I do not want to imply that everyone in my family all the time says, "I'm glad you're doing what you need to do . . . have a nice class tonight!" In fact, there is often one person who expresses the opposite. What has changed is our ability to talk about conflicting needs and feelings.

Notice three things that you can expect in going through these steps of change. One, the steps are continuous and overlapping. Two, you will sometimes make sudden leaps in short spans of time after spending much time in thinking and gathering information. Three, you will go through these steps over and over in the cycle of change. Every time you repeat this process, you will be at different places in the cycle with each of your unwanted patterns. Eventually, you will be able to relax into your process of change and transformation. You will learn to accept the process of breaking out of old, crystallized patterns, and you will anticipate eagerly the joy of new levels of freedom—which feels good!

Steps for Changing:
1. Awareness of problem.
2. Information gathering.
3. No Man's Land.
4. Risk taking time.
5. Resolution and acceptance.

Chapter Two

Self-Esteem: The Foundation

> ... the only true measure of success is the degree that one actually does "feel good" ...
> —L. S. Barksdale, *Building Self-Esteem*

Many of you want to feel good about yourselves but do not know how. The most important aspect of feeling good is loving yourself. Building a solid foundation of sound self-esteem is the first thing that is required for you to feel good. When you unconditionally accept yourself right now, the way you are, you have a solid foundation which will touch every other aspect of your life.

What is self-esteem? What are the characteristics of low and high self-esteem? How do you develop your level of self-esteem?

Self-esteem is the degree that you feel warm and loving toward yourself. It is how you feel about yourself. If you were to measure your self-esteem and you could use a thermometer as an analogy, each degree would be a different level of how you feel about yourself. Everyone has a level of self-esteem that goes beyond the daily shift in moods. If you react emotionally to each event and person in your life, then you have a lower degree or level of self-esteem than someone who does not react as readily to outside events and people.

A common misconception is that self-esteem is your self-image. It is not the pictures you see of yourself in your mind or how you think you should feel. Self-esteem is an emotion. You may be unaware of your feelings and emotions because they cannot be seen or touched. If this is so, then much of your self-esteem is hidden from you and is unconscious. It is to your advantage to become consciously aware of your self-esteem which will clear up many of your problems. You can create your life the way you want it to be. Your health and relationships can improve when you build your self-esteem.

Accepting yourself is the foundation upon which your life is built. Everything that you experience will be colored by your feelings about yourself. Sound self-esteem, therefore, is necessary in order for you to be content with your life and to feel good.

We cannot always determine the symptoms of low self-esteem; however, we can get some clues by noticing extremes in behavior, feelings, and beliefs. Take Lisa, for example. She talks with her hands in front of her face, slumps, speaks very softly, and cannot make eye contact for long. Lisa is suffering from low self-esteem. Her body language and tone of voice tell us this. At the other extreme, Ray talks very loudly and boldly. He continually tells others about his accomplishments, the books he has read, the important people he has met. He gives lots of advice but never listens. Ray is also suffering from low self-esteem.

Other people suffering from low self-esteem are those who put themselves down or brag about themselves or those who are jealous, envious, or untrusting of others. People who are constantly blaming themselves or others, people who have an obsessive desire for money, power, and prestige, or people who are afraid of change and of taking risks have low self-esteem. People who do not communicate, either by holding back with silence or by engaging in endless chatter, also suffer from low self-

SELF-ESTEEM: THE FOUNDATION

esteem. People with a desperate need to win or to be accepted, people who must be "right," and those who fear making mistakes and must always look perfect—all of these have symptoms of low self-esteem.

In addition, there is usually an inner emptiness. Deep inside they know they are not happy or fulfilled. Many times they even admit they do not like themselves. This leaves them little foundation for success in either relationships or a career.

On the other hand, people with sound self-esteem feel okay about themselves and others—they *feel good.* People with sound self-esteem have a warm glow of inner peace and assurance. They have no need to dominate others or to be dominated. Their quiet confidence is sensed by others. They know themselves well and feel comfortable being who they are without judging or blaming themselves. They take responsibility for themselves as well as for their decisions, thoughts, feelings, and actions. Notice that these are qualities of an ideal person. Use this picture as a model in your process of growing towards your own ideal.

How did you get your self-esteem, and where did your sense of self begin? You were most affected by your primary caretakers (usually your mother) during your preschool years. You were like a sponge—totally absorbing the thoughts, feelings, and level of awareness of this person or persons. Your parents or the parental figures who took care of you (older siblings, relatives, and babysitters) communicated their consciousness to you through their relationships with you. You came to know yourself by how others reacted to you, talked to you, held you, and responded to you. Most children value themselves to the degree that they are valued. Your early conditioning or environment reflected to you what your primary caretakers thought and felt about you and about themselves. In your earliest years you had only this external means of validating who you were.

When we live in a healthy society, the impact most people have on their children will be mostly positive.

The fact is that most people have lots of problems, many of which are denied. Since many people have low self-esteem, the problem is perpetuated in the raising of children.

I might add here that some people survived their difficult childhoods better than others. Even as children we have choices. We are not entirely at the mercy of outside influences. It is very rare, however, for a child to have enough maturity and strength to reject the negativity and confusion parents and other adults unwittingly project.

In addition to parents, your peers and teachers gave aspects of themselves to you and further influenced your self-esteem. Other people treated you as they treated themselves. If they were critical of themselves, they were critical of you. It they were able to separate their own behavior from themselves, they were able to forgive you when they did not like your behavior. Depending on the degree of self-esteem these other people had, they projected it onto you. They did this through their feelings, attitudes, tone of voice, communication styles, and interest in you.

Other people's reactions and opinions of you may still be affecting your self-esteem. If this is true for you, it is essential to make a shift from the external validation of who you are (other people's opinions) to an internal sense of who you are. This is the heart of the problem of low self-esteem. This book will further explain how to open the door to self-awareness and know yourself from within. This inner knowing and understanding of yourself is essential to feeling good.

On the other hand, you need not completely eliminate what the outside world is saying about you. Other people's feedback is a source of information to consider; what they say may or may not be true. Check it out before you agree or disagree.

Look again at Lisa. Her mother tells her even as an adult, "You are selfish and self-centered." Lisa is beginning to see that her mother says this whenever she does not get her needs met. Many times it has nothing to do with Lisa. Lisa is learning to detach herself from the words "selfish" and "self-centered." These have been trigger words to her: they have meant that if she were compliant and passive and did what was expected of her, she would be loved. This compliant behavior has always forced Lisa to suppress her angry feelings and to replace them with headaches and feelings of unworthiness. Since she failed to notice or to voice her feelings in response to her mother's comments, these strong emotions imploded in her body.

Lisa is learning to hear the messages her mother is giving rather than believe that the criticism is true. She responds differently now. She may say, "Mom, you have been really working hard lately, and you haven't spent any time on yourself." This usually changes the direction of the conversation and allows her mother to express her frustrations positively without blaming Lisa. During this process Lisa thinks, "Mom is in pain." This helps her to detach from her mother's negative statements which used to create feelings of unworthiness on Lisa's part.

Some other factors contributing to your feelings of self-worth when you were a child were how well you mastered your physical and intellectual environment. Were you able to walk, run, ride a bike, and catch a ball early, or did you do these things late? Did you already know your phone number, address, colors, and ABC's when you entered school, or did you get a slow start? Another important part of your self-esteem is how attractive others thought you were physically and how you felt about your looks. These early interpretations of your physical mastery of your body, your intellectual development, and your physical characteristics still primarily affect your present feelings of worthiness—that is, unless you have already begun the process of self-awareness and are developing an inner perspective of yourself.

Let us look at Fran, who was an unplanned fourth child. Her mother needed to work to support the family because her father was regularly unemployed. Her father and aunt provided her early caretaking, and neither wanted the job. No one held Fran as much as she needed to be held. It was always noisy in her home, and she never felt safe or wanted. In fact, many of her early experiences gave her the impression that she was in the way and a bother; she learned to withdraw for comfort.

Fran's first day at school was very painful. Even now she shudders when she talks about it. The other children already knew their ABC's and she did not. At recess she was afraid to talk to other children and they made fun of her shyness. As you can see, Fran's outer world reflected many messages that she had learned at home such as, "You don't count," and "You are stupid," and "You are unfriendly." Now it is easier to understand why Fran felt so unloved and why she behaved by withdrawing.

Children perceive events and people through the filters of their personal experience. Their perceptions may or may not be accurate, but children commonly make the assumption that something is wrong with themselves or that they are "no good" when other people pull away from them or say mean things to them. Habits of self-perception thus formed in childhood persist unconsciously during adulthood. If you could objectively look at each event that is painful to you, you might find that other people have their own problems; they are often unaware of the effect their words or actions have on you or others.

Now let us look at Ray, an only child. He knew his ABC's before he was two years old. He could ride a bike earlier than his cousin who was a year older than he. But no matter what Ray did as a child, more was expected of him. Rather than compliment him on what he did well, his mother pointed out where he could improve. On the first day of school, Richard, another boy in Ray's class, could beat him at just about everything—counting by twos, doing somersaults in P. E., or riding a bike. Ray was so accustomed to being compared to other children and being the best that he felt "less than" when some-

Self Esteem is

a feeling,

not a mental concept

of who you are.

one outperformed him. Ray's outer world reflected messages to him saying, "You only count when you're the best," or "If you aren't perfect, you are unworthy," and "You have to earn love and praise." It is not surprising that Ray as an adult is constantly bragging and talking about himself in an attempt to gain recognition. He tries to prove he is worthy by convincing everyone else when, in actuality, he is trying to convince himself.

Self-esteem is a feeling and not a mental picture about how you should be. Everyone has a basic level or degree of self-esteem beneath their daily fluctuations of moods. Many people have a concept that their self-esteem is high when they are successful and other people approve of them and that their self-esteem is low when they are out of sorts and nothing seems to be going right. To truly feel you are worthy, you must develop an internal sense of well-being that is not affected by what other people in your life do or say, by how much you accomplish, or by how much you please others. Your feelings about yourself began at, and, some people believe before, your birth. You knew yourself at first only by what the significant others in your life reflected to you and by how they thought and felt about themselves.

Self-esteem is how you feel about yourself. Your base level of self-esteem was conditioned in childhood by the people around you. Sound self-esteem is achieved by increasing your awareness and making corrections to any negativity holding you at a low level of self-esteem.

Today consider taking responsibility for your own level of self-esteem. You no longer have to let your early conditioning determine how you feel. Feeling good is a choice. If you decide that you want to feel good and have sound self-esteem, you have taken the first step necessary to do so. Feeling good based on sound self-esteem is a choice you must first make within your mind before you can experience it.

Chapter Three

Concepts That Build Self-Esteem

Love everyone unconditionally, including yourself.
—Ken Keyes, *Handbook to Higher Consciousness*

To build good feelings about yourself, there are several concepts which are helpful to know, experience, and then understand. You need to change your way of thinking if you want to improve the quality of your life and feel good. These concepts are important to understand and accept before using the techniques presented in Chapter Five to change how you feel about yourself.

1. **ACCEPT YOURSELF RIGHT NOW THE WAY YOU ARE.** It no longer serves you to wait until the future to love yourself. Remember the acorn, you are okay right now. Have you ever heard anyone say, "I'll be happy when I get my degree" or " ... when I lose weight" or " ... when I am a parent," etc.? Then when the person experiences what was supposed to make him or her feel happy, the happiness does not last. That perfect time in the future with the perfect you does not exist. The sooner you learn to accept yourself now as you are with no strings attached, the better you will feel. The

paradox is that this attitude of acceptance is the ingredient required to create what you want in the future.

I once weighed 20 pounds more than I do today. I felt very bad about myself. I spent lots of time missing the joy of the present moment; I focused instead on the future. I would say, "When I am thin, I'll be happy. I'll be able to do thus and so."

When I did lose the weight, I felt happy and bright with all the attention, praise, and acknowledgment I received from others. That lasted only a short time, however. I found I still had to live with myself. Just being thin couldn't make me happy because others were not always around to compliment me and make me feel good about myself. I had to face myself again because I still had the same problems that I had when I was heavier.

I realize now that I was learning lessons in self-esteem. As long as I was dependent on others' acknowledgment that I was attractive at a certain weight, I would have the same low self-esteem that I had before I lost weight. I now realize what a loss it was for me not to have loved myself when I was heavier; I wasted a lot of time waiting for the future to make me happy. I learned also that I had to feel good about myself right now in order to keep the extra weight off.

2. LOOK INSIDE YOURSELF NOT OUTSIDE YOURSELF TO FEEL GOOD. Many of you have been taught to evaluate your self-worth by outer appearances and accomplishments—by your looks, your educational degrees, your cars, your houses, your children, etc. In reality sound self-esteem must come from within you and not from the outer world. "Out there" is dependent on other people, the weather, economic cycles, family, jobs, and a host of other factors. These factors shift and change, and you will be affected by them if you evaluate who you are based on what happens to other people or events outside yourself. "In here" (your thoughts, beliefs, attitudes and perceptions) is the only thing over

which you have complete control. Sound self-esteem emphasizes the inner self that many of us have forgotten with our current lifestyles. There is nothing wrong with achieving; however, the motivation must be to fulfill and to please your inner self. Only when recognition and belief in yourself come from within are you able to accomplish or achieve with real satisfaction. When you achieve for other people's recognition and acceptance, you will not feel satisfied when others are not around to compliment or acknowledge you, and your good feelings about your accomplishment will not last.

Why achieve to gain a sense of recognition and power through others? Is it not of much greater value to know and accept the power that is always potentially within yourself, regardless of your achievements? Achievements coming from this awareness are expressions of yourself and not just the validation of yourself.

At the same time there is nothing wrong with listening to what others say about you and accepting their feedback. In fact, sometimes this is useful. The important thing is that you must ultimately rely on yourself and not on the opinions of other people to feel good about yourself.

The school system contributed to some of my feelings of low self-esteem. Achievement was so important. I have memories of trying so hard and not coming close to getting a high grade. I have memories in elementary school of crying and crying each time a report card came out, around the ages of eight to ten. The system then was not to give A's, B's, and C's, but instead there were four columns which said something like "works up to potential," "acceptable," "needs help," or "unacceptable." Actually, the idea was good—I believe young children do not need grades for feedback on how they are doing. In my own mind at the time, I did not accept the evaluation my teachers gave me which placed many of the checks in the second column. If I was not supposed to be compared to anyone but myself, why didn't they see I was working up to my potential?

I could not put that into words at that time, and in those days not much was being done in the way of active listening, to crack the code of why a child was upset or frustrated; so this was an area my mother and I stumbled through with only moderate success. The recollection contributed to my getting involved with my first daughter's homework around the same age, which I talked about earlier.

I have a more balanced way of looking at achievement now. Take writing this book, for example. It has been a process of growth and unfolding; not just an object to get finished as fast as I can. The value of this growth is that I can now look inside myself and feel good, instead of looking at what I accomplish or at what other people may think of me.

3. STOP JUDGING YOURSELF AND OTHERS. To do this it is helpful to drop "shoulds" and "oughts" from your vocabulary. "Shoulds" and "oughts" are value judgments. Judging yourself or another lowers self-esteem. When you say to another or when you think, "You should . . . ," you really mean, "If I were you, I would . . . " Since no two people have exactly the same early environment, life experiences, genes, etc., it is unfair to expect others to do what you would do in their place. If you use "shoulds" and "oughts" with others, know that you are the hardest on yourself. When you use an "I should" message, you have a mental concept of what you want, but you do not have the skills or awareness to do it yet. We are the hardest on ourselves when we have been able to achieve something in the past and cannot repeat it or maintain it. If we did it once, we "ought" to be able to do it again, right? Know that there are reasons why you are unable at times to do what you think you should. Again, it serves no purpose to beat yourself up mentally when you are unable to do what you wish you could do. It helps to remind yourself that you are working in that direction and that change is a continuing process. It is helpful to ask yourself, "Do I really want to do this, or do

I think I should do this to please another?" It is more relevant to ask yourself, "Will I or won't I do this?"

I once gave a self-esteem lecture for teachers. One teacher asked, "If I don't put 'you should have . . . ' on a student's paper, what do I write?" This is a very important question for people in positions of authority. I believe feedback is important; yet I think only marking errors is perpetuating low self-esteem in others. After finding a positive, you can say, "You could . . . the next time," or "It is helpful to . . . ," or simply state the facts, such as "needs more detail," or "no main idea," or "illegible—neater handwriting required to pass."

4. SEPARATE "YOU" FROM YOUR BEHAVIOR AND ACCOMPLISHMENTS. You are not your behavior. You are the one who behaves. Your behavior is what you do to get your needs met. Your needs motivate you to behave in certain ways. Different people may get the same need met with different behaviors depending on the background of each person. For example, if you ask a room full of people what each would do if his or her car stopped on the freeway, there will be many different responses based on each person's self-awareness and depending on individual needs. One person might lock the car and walk to the nearest telephone, another might hitchhike, and yet another might cry until someone stopped to help.

If you have a behavior that you do not like in yourself, you raise your level of self-esteem by remembering that you are okay even if your behavior is not. If someone close to you behaves in a manner that is unacceptable to you, it is important to communicate that it is their behavior you do not like and that you always love them as a person. People are not bad when they act badly, and neither are you.

5. AVOID COMPARING AND COMPETING WITH OTHERS. Competition and comparison are part of most people's upbringing. Most of our schools, sports, jobs, and

parenting styles are set up this way. There is a current belief that competition and comparison are healthy and necessary. However, the way we use competition tends to produce low self-esteem. When you compare yourself with someone else, there will always be a winner and a loser. Life is not a race; we all get there in our own way and in our own time.

It serves no purpose for there to be two people exactly alike on the planet. Therefore, competing to be the same or better than another is missing the point of life! There is a special place for each and every one of us.

We do need standards of excellence, though, and our system works by acknowledging and rewarding those people who achieve high standards. If you are in competition with a person who achieves a high standard of excellence, you may feel put down when your achievements are compared with his or hers. Consider that we all win whenever another achieves a goal or a standard of excellence. If you do compete (and this is how life is set up), just remember not to be addicted to winning. Enjoy the game of life.

Again I will illustrate with writing this book. It would serve no useful purpose for me not to have written it just because there are dozens of other self-help books. I could have talked myself out of writing it because I am not an expert or because I cannot spell. Instead it is coming from within me. It may or may not be a best seller. It feels good simply to create what comes from within me. I now write regardless of whether anyone else reads it or likes it or uses the information. I have discovered that one of my talents is expressing ideas, and it feels good to use it.

I believe everyone has at least one gift and it will serve you to find out what it is. It does not matter whether your gift makes you Number One in some widely appreciated activity, or just makes you quite good at something not generally appreciated. It can be an abstract gift like being able to understand what other people (or

Awareness is the first step in change.

animals) are feeling or communicating. It does not matter whether or not it has competitive value.

6. KNOW THAT YOU ARE ALWAYS DOING YOUR BEST. This is a difficult concept for many people to accept. Just for a moment consider it as a possibility. Remember that each person has a different level of awareness based on his/her early programming, life experiences, beliefs, genes, etc. You can act only out of your current level of awareness to meet your current needs. If your needs are unconscious, you may be surprised at some of your behavior. When you are unhappy with your behavior, even if you have been capable of acting the way you wanted to in the past, it is helpful to look at your needs. Some of your needs may be competing with each other, and some of them may be unhealthy. When you become aware of your hidden needs, you will see the conflicts that keep you stuck doing things you do not like to do.

Barb wants to lose weight, and she cannot figure out why she keeps eating. In therapy she learns that she has competing needs. One need is to lose weight; however, a more dominant need is to feel emotionally secure. Food has become the means for satisfying her security need; therefore, she eats. The dominant need wins. It serves no purpose for Barb to be angry and blame herself for not losing weight. She is doing the best she can until she discovers new information about these competing needs and other unconscious needs that may be motivating her. She is learning to look for constructive ways to satisfy her emotional hunger rather than eating. Barb often calls a friend in her support group and talks when she is not really hungry for food but does need to dissipate an attack of the munchies.

7. PRACTICE UNCONDITIONAL LOVING. It is important to learn to love unconditionally in order to feel good about yourself. (Substitute the word "accept" if "love" is not comfortable). Unconditional love is what

the Greeks called *agape* love—love that has no reasons and no boundaries. It simply is love given without any expectations of a return. Conditional love, on the other hand, has to be earned, and there are expectations placed on either yourself or on the person to whom you are relating in order to be loved.

Examples of conditional love are, "I would love myself if I were thinner or if I had more money." "I love you as long as you meet my expectations and please me." With unconditional love you are worthy simply because you exist. There are no reasons for this love and acceptance. In the process of learning to love unconditionally, you need to see where you have placed expectations on your love, and then you need to let go of them. It is an ingredient of sound self-esteem to love yourself unconditionally first, because this will allow you to love others unconditionally.

This sounds logical, and you might wonder what gets in the way of people loving unconditionally. The answer is fear. People can act only one of two ways—out of love or out of fear. When people are fearful, it colors their attempts at clear, clean, unconditional loving. This is very tricky sometimes. The outer behaviors of people may look right and yet feel off. This is a clue that there is a "hook" in the gift or expression of love.

Let me illustrate this concept with Mike, who was not sure whether or not he wanted to go to college. His parents initiated therapy so that he might get some direction and motivation in choosing a major college. As Mike grew in therapy, it became clear that he was not motivated to go to college at all. Mike's father said that he would accept Mike's choice and would support Mike in a decision to find a job.

But Mike's decision not to go to college brought out a pattern in his father that had not been obvious at first. He gave subtle messages to Mike in his body language and by his tone of voice indicating that he disapproved of Mike's decision. Also he began distancing himself from Mike emotionally. On the surface nothing was wrong.

Mike's father was giving him the financial opportunity to go to college and was providing him with therapy to gain the motivation. But when Mike made his choice and the decision was different from his father's expectations, the father then placed conditions on his giving and pulled away from Mike emotionally. Hidden fears blocked Mike's father from unconditionally accepting his son's choice. He had grown up poor and had worked his way to affluence. He wanted his son to reap the benefits of his hard work and not have to suffer. Even though fear for his son's future was in the back of his mind, he eventually let go and allowed Mike to live his own life.

And even though he did make mistakes, Mike needed the freedom to experience life for himself. Unconditional love was the lesson Mike's father needed to learn. When the father let go of his fears for Mike and allowed his son to make his own mistakes, Mike was freed from the bondage that conditional love had placed upon him. Now Mike and his father have a healthy adult relationship where there is acceptance and a way for each to live his own life without either having to please the other.

8. NO ONE IS TO BLAME FOR YOUR UNHAPPINESS. This may be one of the most powerful points in the book, and the most difficult to let go of. We all compile lists of grievances against others and against ourselves. Know that when you blame others, you are many times even harder on yourself. Blame and guilt lower self-esteem and are demotivators in the process of change and growth. Many people beginning the self-growth path blame their parents for their "mistakes" in child rearing. It serves no purpose to blame your parents or anyone else; remember that everyone is doing the best he is capable of doing with his level of awareness. Going beyond blame and guilt requires you to make peace with every person in your life who has ever upset, betrayed, or victimized you. You do this through acceptance, love, and forgiveness. The type of forgiveness that I mean is not the type where you pretend you are mature, look down

upon the person who has wronged you, and let them off the hook. Instead, I mean understanding how and why the other person could do what they did. You realize you forgive them because they really did not do anything to you. They were merely acting out their life dramas with their own perceptions which may have been distorted and unhealthy. This is simple to explain intellectually and very difficult to practice. You may need to release a lot of anger and pain before getting to this place of forgiveness. For example, some people scream into a pillow or in the shower, and this releases some of the tension. Other people get their anger out by hitting a pillow or kick bag. Some people cry, others talk to a friend or to a counselor, and others write angry letters in a journal and do not send them.

James was abused by his parents, had a sadistic doctor as a child, and had a parochial education full of physical and emotional abuse when there was not total compliance with the highly restrictive rules. Much of James' adult life revolved around his fear of bullies and his concern with protecting himself. The career he created was full of ruthless, dominating people who continued to reflect back to him his early patterns of victimization. It took James more than three years of intense therapy to overcome these patterns.

James was full of rage and blame for his parents, former teachers, former and current co-workers, and employers. He learned on his own the therapeutic value of hitting a kick bag, a technique that gave him a physical outlet for his mental and emotional pain. In therapy he began to make peace with his parents, which affected most of his other relationships in life. He learned intellectually that his parents were not intentionally out to get him; they had just been ignorant of how to be nurturing, compassionate parents. During his second year of therapy with me, James finally validated this new knowledge emotionally by writing letters to his elderly father. His first fifteen letters were not acceptable to mail. They were full of blame, hate, and anger. Gradually the poison was released, and James wrote and mailed a long letter to his father. It has turned his life around.

His father was so happy with the letter that he shared his interpretation of James' childhood. This began the process of forgiveness and allowed James to see what motivated his father. James is now learning to forgive other authority figures from his past, and this frees him daily from feeling victimized when someone reminds him of his painful past.

When you move beyond blaming others and feeling guilty, you free yourself. It feels good to learn and grow from mistakes instead of staying stuck and feeling bad. It makes sense to look at what you do not like in yourself or in your relationships and to think about what you can do differently to make changes. Blame and guilt are stuck places. Learning from past mistakes and choosing to make changes helps you to feel free from the past. Take responsibility for changing what you do not like, and you will begin to feel better about yourself.

If these ideas are new or difficult to understand, you may need to ponder them before you can accept them. The insights they offer can change your guiding beliefs about yourself and about how life operates, greatly improving your emotional well-being. Remember that building sound self-esteem is a process of learning to love and accept yourself as you are. This emotional change is what feeling good is all about.

Concepts that Build Self Esteem

1. Accept yourself right NOW.
2. Look inside yourself not outside.
3. Stop judging yourself and others.
4. Separate "you" from your behavior.
5. Avoid comparing and competing.
6. Know that you are doing your best.
7. Practice unconditional loving.
8. Stop blaming; take responsibility for your life.

Chapter Four

True and False Guiding Beliefs

> Our attitudes determine whether we experience peace or fear, whether we are well or sick, free or imprisoned.
> —Gerald Jampolsky, *Teach Only Love*

You have a set of assumptions about life, human behavior, God, relationships, and yourself. I call these assumptions guiding beliefs, or rules you live your life by. Many of these beliefs are unconscious to you, and you do not remember ever having learned them. Yet these are the beliefs that guide your life.

Many of your guiding beliefs are not true and yet they are strongly influencing your life. When you become aware of your guiding beliefs, you can reduce and finally eliminate any of them that restrict you and make you feel bad. What we believe to be true is true for us even if the belief is false. For example, you may believe that if you go outside in the winter with wet hair, you will catch a cold. This is true if you believe it, and there is a good chance you will catch a cold when you go outside with wet hair. Another person might have the opposite belief and would probably not get a cold by going outside in the winter with wet hair. In both cases, it would not matter what other people might say contrary to your position (unless you are about ready to change your guiding belief). You know that you are right because you have proven it to yourself. Remember that both positions are true for the persons believing them. The challenge is to discover and live greater truths.

It is necessary to consciously know what your guiding beliefs are if you want to learn to feel good about yourself. These beliefs are creating your interpretation of the events in your life and your reality. Some beliefs may be false and may be unhealthy for you.

I suggest you stop reading at this time, close your eyes and think about your personal guiding beliefs. Then open your eyes and make a list of them.

You were NOT taught some desirable guiding beliefs that are true; you WERE taught some undesirable ones that are NOT true. Notice as you read this section which of the following ideas make you uncomfortable or which ones you react to. These areas in your belief system may give you clues as to why you have blocked your ability to feel good. It is not important that you agree or disagree. Simply consider these ideas even if they feel uncomfortable to you. The following examples are ideas that may be influencing some of your beliefs, or they may actually be some of your guiding beliefs. Let us begin with beliefs that many of you were NOT taught.

1. YOU ARE WORTHY AND DESERVING OF LOVE. You may have been taught that you are unworthy and that you have to earn your worthiness among others. Even some religious teachings reinforce this state of conditional love. If your home or your church (or both) taught you that you do not count and that you are unlovable until proven lovable, this concept may be difficult for you to accept. Know that there are religions and people in the world today who teach the opposite. Remember you are innately good and worthy of love. To reach the realization within yourself that this is true, you may

need to study and contemplate the teachings of other philosophies and religions. You may need to meet someone who loves you unconditionally, a friend, teacher, or counselor. Eventually you will feel from within that you are good simply because you are a part of the "All-That-Is," God or Good: that because you exist you are worthy.

Recently I had a student who just could not get this concept. After several attempts, I used this analogy, which really addressed him. I asked him to see a newborn baby in his mind. He smiled and could do this. As he looked, I talked about this baby and how it is deserving of love, affection and attention—for no reason other than because it exists. He said, "Yes, I can see now what you are saying about worthiness."

Next I asked him to imagine himself as that baby. That did it ... he smiled and looked softer and more relaxed. "I get it," he said quietly.

2. IT IS ALL RIGHT AND GOOD TO LOVE YOURSELF. You are not selfish and conceited if you love yourself. You deserve love simply because you exist. When you accept and love yourself, you have the inner resources and strength to handle everything that life presents to you. You come from a place of being grounded and being filled up rather than from a place of weakness and emptiness. You are able to give to others instead of hoping and expecting others to fill you up with love. You can give only what you have. This was hard for me to practice because I had a guiding belief that said, "I can do what I want, or do something for myself only after everyone else's needs in my family are met."

I remember clearly my 34th birthday, when I felt the most unhappy. That was rock bottom for me. I was empty. It was difficult to give. I was needy; but at the time I had to give so much. My children were ages ten, six, and two. I had created a life of being available and giving, yet I felt that I had nothing left. Needless to say, it was an intense time in my marriage.

I became aware of things that nurtured me. My teaching was probably number one—students appreciated what I had to offer in the way of insight rather than depending on me for various wants. Also there were a handful of close friends; with them I was simply loved and accepted.

The gift my husband gave me about that time was to take my youngest daughter to visit our families in the East for a week at Thanksgiving. This was significant for several reasons. I had been unable to separate for long from my older two children at that age because I believed a good mother was there for her young children. Yet I had wanted more participation from my husband in parenting, and here he was willing to participate in a most thoughtful way. Could I let go of my old beliefs that children need a primary caretaker to be there *all* the time in order to grow up healthy and secure?

I had one of the best weeks of my life. I remember sitting in front of the fireplace reading *The Road Less Traveled* and pondering and thinking much of the time. I even took the older two children (who, by the way, played together happily almost the whole week) out for Thanksgiving dinner. This was quite a contrast to another family dinner I will describe later, which was "ruined" for me only because I expected everyone to enjoy celebrating the traditional season in the same way I wanted to.

I learned during this period that it was not only okay but was a requirement for me to fill myself up if I were going to be able to truly give to others.

3. IT IS OKAY TO MAKE MISTAKES AND NOT BE PERFECT. If you were perfect, you would not need to be here. This is the school of life. When you correct your mistakes, you learn. I like the definition of perfection given by Ken Carey in *Vision*. According to Carey, "Perfection is not never making a mistake; perfection is never consciously making a mistake."

I used to have many ideas about how I "should" be. I was most unforgiving whenever I goofed up. Take the illustration above: a perfect mother cannot only give. She must nourish and feed herself as well. I made "mistakes" because I was unaware, not because I was bad or was not a perfect expression of myself.

4. FEELINGS ARE OKAY. Emotions such as anger and depression are not wrong or bad; they simply are. You can use anger, jealousy, or depression to feel bad; or you can see them as symptoms of problems, become aware of the causes, and use the emotional energy to make changes in your life. Anger, for example, is considered a secondary emotion. The feelings behind anger are the primary problem. These feelings could include fear, insecurity, loss of control, or fear of abandonment.

I did not know what a feeling was until I was 30 years of age. I had felt all the time—in fact, this is my primary mode. I would get a lump in my throat, have an upset stomach, be nervous and cry; yet I did not know what emotions I was feeling. A great awakening came to me during a Marriage Encounter weekend with my husband. Here I learned to put to words what I felt, and learned to communicate them.

5. USE YOUR TALENTS. This was discussed earlier and I want to emphasize it because it has been an important key for my own good feelings. Developing, enjoying, and sharing your talents makes you feel good about yourself. I'm using the word "talent" loosely; for example, it can mean the ability to listen to others or to work with animals or to care for plants. It feels good to share your talents. If the people now in your life do not accept or need what you have to give, there are many others who do.

Volunteer work is one way to meet people who need what you have to offer. I would go a step further and say that volunteer work where you practice your gifts and talents is really not work at all, because you receive as much as you give. I developed my confidence in speaking and giving workshops by volunteering at the Houston

Center for Attitudinal Healing. You can do something similar. Just think about what you love to do, practice the skills by volunteering, and create yourself into a job where you get paid for what you love to do.

If you are in a job that does not use your talents, volunteering to use your abilities is one way to create another job—a job that does use your talents, a job that you'll enjoy. It feels good to do that!

6. ALL BEHAVIOR MAKES SENSE. If you do not like your behavior or another's, you can look behind the actions to see what is motivating you or the other person to act. Your needs motivate you. When you are surprised or disappointed at your own behavior, remember that you have competing needs. You may be unaware of some need you have brushed aside for a long time. As you become conscious of suppressing needs that are demanding expression, you will find ways to meet your needs instead of blaming yourself when they erupt in unwanted behavior. Remember Barb, who tried unsuccessfully to lose weight until her need for security was met by talking to a friend? Afterward, she was able to stay on a diet; but until she realized and found ways to satisfy her need for security, her behavior made no sense. The more aware you are of your real needs, the easier it is to understand and to change your unwanted behaviors. Begin by seeking insight into your needs, not focusing on your behaviors.

I would like to share with you an example from my family. One Sunday morning, Lindy, my oldest daughter, came into my room and began, "I can't believe I acted like Sarah when I was her age. It was so hard to babysit last night for Sarah. She wouldn't listen to me, wouldn't go to bed, and she kicked and hit Faye (Lindy's friend)." I listened for awhile and then decided it was time to confront Sarah, who was watching TV while eating breakfast in the kitchen.

"Sarah," I said, "I hear you had some bad behavior last night."

"I didn't," she denied (a normal age seven response).

"Well, Lindy tells me you hit and kicked Faye. If you are going to be abusive and hurt other people, then I will have to punish your bad behavior."

I had her immediate attention, then. She said, "Like what?"

I answered, "Like no playing with your friends for awhile." She knew this must be serious.

Then I asked, "Why did you act like that?" I was surprised at how easily she responded, "Because Faye's always over here and I wanted to be with Lindy." (I did not answer her with logic; I just listened, and responded to the feeling level).

"You were jealous of Faye getting all of Lindy's attention?" I clarified.

"Yes, I wanted Lindy to play with me," she went on.

Lindy came into the kitchen and I said, "Lindy, did you hear why Sarah was mean to Faye last night?"

The two of them talked a minute and then Sarah left the room.

Lindy and I looked at each other and Lindy said, "Wow, that was incredible!"

I said, "Did you see how active listening helped crack the code of her behavior?" And Lindy just nodded.

I then got tears in my eyes and said, "I didn't know how to do that with you—that's probably one reason why you cried so much." Then we were hugging. "That's okay, Mom," was all Lindy said.

I said, "We're healing the past, aren't we? Maybe you won't have to deal with the same problems in coping with your kids because you understand active listening."

Then we heard Sarah call from the other room saying Faye was on the phone for Lindy. After a few moments, Lindy said, "Mom, guess what Sarah just did? She called Faye and apologized!"

I had to jump up and down for joy. So much had been healed for us all at that moment.

All behavior makes sense when we find out what needs are motivating ourselves and others. When we identify the needs, we have choices about how to get those needs met so we aren't surprised by negative behavior. Again, it is necessary to see the behavior as separate from the essence of the person. The nature of the individual is essentially good, even when his/her behavior is inappropriate.

7. PEOPLE ARE YOUR MIRRORS. If you do not like another person's behavior, it is because you do not like a part of yourself. An example of this mirror concept is the defense mechanism (where we defend ourselves from ourselves) called projection. We want to be "good," so we disown anything that does not fit into our image of good and project it onto someone else whom we then label "bad." This means we have made the judgment that a certain behavior or feeling or attitude is bad—so bad that it could not be a part of us—and we deny and suppress that part of ourselves to avoid facing and dealing with it as our own. When we do this, we are missing an opportunity to grow and to become more conscious of ourselves.

When I do not like someone's behavior I ask myself many questions to see what I can learn about myself. What lesson do I need to learn from this situation? Who does this person remind me of in the past? What am I expecting or demanding from him/her? Why do I care? Am I hiding that same behavior from myself? Am I unconsciously doing it somewhere in my life? How does this fit into any of my patterns? What do I need that I am not getting that this person is bringing now to my conscious awareness?

I can illustrate this best by an example from my own life. Once I had an acquaintance whose behavior really got on my nerves. She had two maids, few routine demands were made on her, and she was totally focused on her daughter, an only child. I heard time and again about this child's ability to read at age five (I also had a five year old), and what her wonderful IQ scores were. I kept bumping into this woman, and each time found myself irritated and upset by these recitations. The old me was jealous that she had it so easy and had such a bright kid. "Why couldn't I get a smart, compliant child," I would think. (This all happened during the homework crisis period with my older daughter, which magnified the stress.) You can see how patterns tend to overlap, and eventually crash into each other until you catch on.

The new me knew there was something being offered for my growth, disguised as dislike for this other person's behavior. I began to ponder and look inside myself. I discovered that I was not using my talents, either. I was living through my kids, too, trying to be fulfilled only by mothering and homemaking. What this showed me that I needed to do is described in detail in the introduction of this book. I needed to teach. I needed people who needed what I had to offer, helping them develop their self-awareness. Since I had done such a good job creating a lifestyle in which everyone needed me at home, it was difficult—and risky—to be away in the evenings. But this I finally did for my own emotional survival, and it was not a disaster for my loved ones who at first had resisted the change in our set patterns. It was a positive move for us all. It's funny, I rarely run into this person whose behavior used to irritate me so much; I'm too busy with my life to care about her life.

This also works in a positive direction. When you like another, it is because that person reflects something you like in yourself, or something you want to develop in yourself. You do not see anything in another unless it is a part of yourself, at least potentially. As you learn to accept yourself, you will grow to accept all people regardless of their behavior. This does not imply that you have to be around those people you do not like. Just learn from them and work on yourself, not them.

I believe that in the process of change and growth, it is very important to "hang around" people who reflect love, acceptance, support, interest, and caring. This can come from a friend, a therapist, or a support group. I have found that joining a support group is the way many people get the strength and courage to go forward. This is especially so when there is no support and encouragement to draw from in their daily lives.

8. YOU CREATE YOUR OWN LIFE, AND YOU ALONE ARE RESPONSIBLE FOR YOURSELF. Most of you were not taught that when you focus your thoughts, you put energy into creating those thoughts. The stronger your thoughts and images feel the more powerful your creations are. They can be negative or positive. What you fear, you create as a goal because you spend so much time thinking about it. The good news is that if you do not like what you have created, you can change it. There is an unwritten law that requires you to use this power only for yourself. It is not to be used to create for other people—no matter how good your intentions are. However, you can align yourself with what another person is creating and add your power to what he/she wants to create. In other words, each person is responsible for his/her own life. It is actually possible to delay another person's growth by attempting to fix or change him/her or to take away his/her pain. The best way to help another is to work on yourself because you have an effect on those around you.

I read once that you can ask children around age seven how their lives will go as grown-ups and many of them can tell you. Eric Berne calls this a "life script." Many of us took on someone else's script for us at an early age. It happens when parents try vicariously to live through their children rather than enjoy their own lives.

I once had a client who, rather than develop her own talents, focused on her son's playing the violin. Even in pre-school this child endured a very regimented schedule in order to become accomplished at the violin. When a trip or activity was in conflict with his routine, the mother would faithfully take the violin along and control the time so that her son never missed a practice period. The power struggles that finally arose brought the two of them in for therapy; and happily, the mother did eventually let go of meeting her own needs for accomplishment and esteem through the child. She finally saw there are healthier ways to develop musical talent, and she realized it had been unfair to ask the child to fulfill her life's needs while she had ignored his.

It is time to take responsibility for creating your own life, to live your own purpose and fulfill your own needs. When you do this, it *feels good.*

Things You Were Not Taught That Are True

1. **You are worthy and deserving of love.**
2. **It is good to love yourself.**
3. **It is ok to make mistakes.**
4. **Feelings are good.**
5. **Your talents are to be used.**
6. **All behavior makes sense.**
7. **People are your mirrors.**
8. **You create your life.**

Now, let us look at some things that many of you were taught that are NOT true.

1. YOU CANNOT GET WHAT YOU WANT IN LIFE (FALSE). Many of you learned that you are not worthy and will never be good or perfect enough to receive what you need and want in life. Since you do not question this false teaching, you do not ask for what you want; you still believe that you do not deserve it. Yet the opposite is true. Remember, you are worthy simply because you exist. You cannot earn your worthiness. You have to accept your worthiness. You can still let your needs and wants be known, even though you think you are not perfect and, therefore, not deserving. The truth is that you can have whatever you are willing and able to accept in life; what you are willing and able to accept is based on your attitudes and guiding beliefs about deserving. Therefore, if you have been taught that you cannot get what you want in life, begin a correction at the guiding belief level that allows you to accept what you ask for. At the very least, consider the *possibility* of receiving what you want.

When I become conscious of something I want to experience, express, own, or become, I first let it be a possibility. I go through my process of why I can't have it or don't deserve it. Then I begin talking back to myself. I ask myself why I want this. Is it worth working or striving for? Can I see in my mind that I will enjoy it in the future? Is it possible I would be burdened by it?

Once I've determined I want it and would receive value from creating it, I begin talking to myself again. For example, when I went to graduate school, I heard people say, "Don't go into counseling; the field is flooded. It's so competitive. You can't get a decent job without a doctoral degree." But when I decided a counseling career was a

TRUE AND FALSE GUIDING BELIEFS

possibility and I wanted it, I would say things to myself like, "Even if there is a shortage of jobs, I may as well be the one who finds one. If anyone can find a job with just a master's degree, I will."

2. EXPECTATIONS ALWAYS ENABLE YOU TO GET WHAT YOU WANT (FALSE). Unrealistic expectations set you up for disappointment. This may sound like a conflict with what was just said; however, realize that you can go to the opposite extreme and demand too much. Living from either extreme blocks you. There is a place of thinking in expanded consciousness where two opposites are both true; this is called a paradox. You must always ask for what you want; however, let go of the outcome and do not force a specific conclusion. For example, you may be working on prosperity consciousness and find that results do not manifest as you expected. There is a clue here that you are inwardly blocking yourself with your guiding beliefs again. You may secretly believe that you are unworthy and, therefore, undeserving. It is helpful to look at what is realistic at this time and make the adjustment. Ask for what you want and let it happen the way it will. Do not assume that you know the best way. It can be a mental trap to force a result before you have removed the blocks that prevent you from being able to achieve what you say you want.

Expectations of others also set you up for disappointments. You have no right to use your control over others; this is a misuse of power. An example is using guilt or punishment to force a particular response or action from another. When you allow others to live and create their own lives, you will find sometimes that what you expect and what the other person can or is willing to do does not always match up. Again, look at what is realistic.

Let me illustrate with an example from my life. I remember one Christmas feeling awful because I had some expectations of what my family would do to support me in creating a wonderful turkey dinner. I wanted to create a day and a holiday meal reminiscent of my childhood. Instead of help, I received constant demands from my youngest daughter, Sarah, aged eighteen months. It seemed that she was no longer cute to her older sisters; she only wanted to take toys apart and undress Barbie dolls. When no one wanted to play with her, Sarah learned a new skill. She learned to climb up and turn on the stove!

Keeping an eye on Sarah was only part of my irritation. That was the Christmas my husband bought the family an Atari and several games for the TV set. He played for four hours straight. While I prepared the dinner, I was constantly interrupted by questions from my two older daughters about how to work new craft kits and games. "How do you play this game?" "How does this work?" By the time dinner was ready, I was worn out and angry. The finale was that the three children did not want any of the food that I had prepared except the cranberry sauce.

I finally figured out what was wrong. I had expected that everyone would help, enjoy, and eat a traditional dinner. In actuality I was the only one who wanted the dinner. No one else cared about dinner. I had set myself up for disappointment, resentment, and anger when other people did not behave as I had expected.

When you find that you have expectations, and we all do, then communicate to the other person what you need and want. Ask, then let go of whether the other person can meet your expectations. Sometimes they can, and sometimes they cannot. It is helpful to question their needs and wants and listen to their expectations. The bottom line is that you must learn to accept the reality of the situation. Some things cannot be changed just by wanting the change.

3. **GET YOUR WANTS MET BEFORE YOUR NEEDS (FALSE).** In our society there is heavy emphasis on material measures of happiness. Often you are trapped into

achieving or trying to get some object without realizing that really you are starving emotionally or spiritually. Rather than a new dress or a new car or eating sweets, what you may need is attention; you may just need someone to care about you, to listen to you, and to enjoy you. Or you may need direction in life in order to feel a sense of purpose. Your needs must be met before you can feel good. The next time you are driven to eat or buy something, stop and ask yourself what you really need.

In the turkey dinner illustration, I was not focusing on what my needs were. I needed to show and express love and to feel connected to my family. Fixing the perfect dinner was how I wanted to express this love. There were other ways to do this, like putting my heart into answering the children's questions and fixing a simple dinner. To connect to the individuals in my family, I needed to respond to what was important to them. It would have been easier to simply be available, to watch my toddler, and play games with the older two children. I did not stop to realize then that there would be lots of years to fix traditional dinners when the children would be grown up enough to participate with enthusiasm.

4. YOU ARE A VICTIM; PEOPLE DO THINGS TO HURT YOU (FALSE). In reality, it is your interpretation of their behavior that makes you feel taken advantage of and not the behavior itself. Let us look at Janice to see how she feels victimized by her husband and see if she really is. Janice entered therapy because she felt depressed and lonely. Whenever she questioned her husband, Ted, in depth about his feelings, he would pull away from her physically and emotionally. The more she tried to create intimacy by sharing her new knowledge about herself and how she wanted to relate differently to him, the further Ted moved away. He would not answer her questions; he just got angry. He would make fun of Janice's therapy and was not interested in sex. Janice interpreted Ted's behavior as rejection. In therapy Janice learned the parallel between her father and her hus-

band. She unconsciously felt the same way that she did when she was a child. When she demonstrated "bad" or unacceptable behavior, her father pulled away from her emotionally. In order to work out of the victim pattern, Janice needed to see that her husband was in pain and that he was afraid to look at problems. Rather than being able to say, "I'm scared," or "I need to think about that," or "I need help," he pulled into an emotionally safe space where he was not affectionate or caring toward Janice. With her new understanding, Janice now sees that Ted does not intentionally set out to hurt her. He simply is not aware of his feelings and inner conflicts. Because she can see that he is in pain, she no longer feels victimized. The interesting thing in this common scenario is that Ted, if you asked him, would say he feels victimized by Janice. Again, this is a paradox. When you can see that both sides are at once true and not true, you can move out of the victim/victimizer pattern of thinking.

5. YOU HAVE TO GO TO CHURCH TO HAVE A RELATIONSHIP WITH GOD (FALSE). Actually, this is one of many beliefs you may have learned from well-intentioned religious teachings, and it can be very scary to question religious beliefs. You may have experienced a period of guilt if you separated from early religious teachings in your life. The degree that your early upbringing was autonomous and gave you permission to question and explore is the degree of guilt that you felt. You formed many of your beliefs and opinions about God by how you were treated by the authority figures in your life, mainly your parents.

It is of primary importance to develop a personal relationship with the Universe, the Source, or God on the journey to feeling good. This needs to take place regardless of your beliefs about God or religion. To know that there is a power greater than yourself is mandatory if you are to feel good about yourself. This power exists all the time and does not depend upon a church or its dogma. The churches and rules were designed to serve and lead people who needed or wanted help to their Source. If you feel you must be in a church or in a certain religion in order to experience this power and if you are unfilled spiritually, then I urge you to explore, question, and experience other aspects of life. For example, explore different religions, learn to meditate, go on a retreat, spend time in nature, or spend time alone each day pondering life.

This power can be concrete and part of a religion, or it can be very abstract where a sense of the unity of all things is felt and God is called Energy or Mother Nature. What is important is to get a personal connection to the greater whole, a sense of purpose and meaning as to why you are here. If this is not yet part of your experience, just know that this connection is possible. As you explore and increase your awareness of yourself, you will one day experience this power greater than yourself, even though you may not believe it now.

A relationship with God (substitute Universe, All That Is, or the Source, if you choose) exists whether you are conscious of it or not. It exists 24 hours a day, inside or outside of a church or system of teaching about God.

I used to be very religious. I *tried* very hard to be "good" and to understand how the Bible was important for my life. It upset me when I got to college, a good place for philosophical debates, and found some people treated the Bible as merely a history book. It had never crossed my mind. I was forced at this time to question my own beliefs, and it was a mini-crisis for me. For a while I did not know what I believed. I read about other religions, visited various churches, and listened to all kinds of viewpoints about God and the universe.

I remember being impacted by a couple whom I met at a weekend get-together at a lake house. They had a baby with four different birth defects, and they amazed me with their acceptance and understanding of what the significance and purpose of this experience was for the three of them. They told me about Edgar Cayce and his ideas about life and healing. I think the first book of his I read was *There Is A River*.

Later, in my twenties, I met a couple in my neighborhood who had an ill daughter with a degenerative nerve disease who was in a state institution for care. I became very close to them and one day offered to go with the mother to visit her daughter. This was a real turning point in my life. On a physical level, there was nothing—no response, no recognition. But on a non-physical level I could feel something very significant; I could feel the bond and the relating and the awareness between them. From that day forward, I have known that there is a spiritual, non-physical part to ourselves. To me, this experience validated God, though I perceived it just as feeling, not as something I could express in logical words.

This feeling has developed in my life over the years. I have learned to have a personal relationship with the Source, and I am growing at my own pace in this process. I keep expanding my awareness of the greater whole and my place in it. There is no limit to God, and no limit to what I may experience in this quest for understanding.

6. YOU WILL FEEL GOOD WHEN YOU HAVE THE "RIGHT" JOB, MATE, CAR, ETC. (FALSE). This is the guiding premise of this book. You have low self-esteem when you validate yourself through other people or by your outer world. Sound self-esteem is the feeling of total acceptance and love for yourself as you are, regardless of what you may now see as your faults, problems, or mistakes, regardless of your looks, weight, race, or IQ. Self-esteem is a quiet, comfortable place of enjoying being who you are. It is knowing who you *really* are: your Self. You have been told that accomplishments and outer appearances determine your level of self-esteem. Again, the opposite is true. When you determine your self-esteem from your appearance, grades, cars, income, or children's behavior, you turn your power to feel good over to another. There is so much pressure to compare and compete, however, that you have to train yourself to go

beyond outer appearances in order to validate who you are. The reason you feel bad when you don't like your weight, your color, your educational level, or your job is that you have forgotten they are not who you are. Remember that you are a precious being. You are an expression of God or the Universe, and you are experiencing and learning life's lessons. You are innately worthy and do not have to earn your reason for being. As you get to know, love, and accept yourself on the inside, outer expressions of you will change. You will like your job, your choice of clothes, and your relationships. Remember, you are the Self or Source expressing in the physical world that is learning and growing.

7. MISTAKES ARE BAD (FALSE). You are in the school of life and are learning lessons daily that move you on course toward your life purpose and goals. Mistakes happen because you do not know or understand something and are unable at that moment to do anything else. When you find that you are repeating a pattern and making the same mistake over and over, it is not that you are weak willed or bad; it simply means that you are unaware of something. The discomfort of the repeated experience will eventually give you the impetus to gather information, to try something different, and finally to become conscious of more parts of yourself.

Mistakes that you are aware of are very valuable because they give you something specific to work on. Really big mistakes are opportunities to learn really big and valuable lessons; if you interpret mistakes this way, you can appreciate them.

I still hear from that perfectionist part inside me who critically reports on a regular basis that I'm doing this or that all wrong. I have conversations with this part of myself to reeducate her. I remind her I'm doing the best I can. Though I do want to do this differently, I don't yet know how, and I can't be held accountable for something I am ignorant about. I gather information and meditate and ponder and eventually visualize it differently. Treating mistakes as opportunities to become more conscious is a more comfortable place to live than criticizing and blaming ourselves. Even with sound self-esteem, you will still make mistakes and have challenges; but you'll look at your mistakes and interpret them differently—more constructively.

8. IT IS BETTER TO GIVE THAN TO RECEIVE (FALSE). For some people it is negative to receive. They have been taught only to give and to serve others. But this works only when they are filled up emotionally. If they do not have their needs met, their giving will be off-center or crooked, and there will be hooks in the gift, a hidden element of expecting something in return.

Look at the example of Ann, whose mother gave her money with a hidden expectation of keeping Ann near her for security. Ann was 35 years old when she decided to deal with this difficult situation in her life. She was no longer comfortable receiving money from her mother, Dorothy, even though she could use it to pay bills. There was a hook when she took the money. Ann felt obligated to call her mother several times a week and to eat dinner there every Sunday. But Ann learned to say no to these gifts and freed herself from their burdensome expectations.

Dorothy had no interests or hobbies. She had only been happy when her children were living with her or when they visited her. She felt lonely and unloved after they left home, and she expected Ann to visit her often. Ann had trouble at first in saying no to her mother and in taking the initiative to change this pattern. But she did change. She began to limit her phone calls and her visits, and her initial discomfort was well worth the effort. Taking this risk produced positive changes even for the mother. Dorothy, out of desperation, began volunteering at a local hospital. Because she was truly needed there, many of her own needs were met through volunteer work. These needs had formerly just been covered up while she clung to her earlier behavior patterns and treated Ann like a dependent child.

Dorothy now has a wholesome outlet for her need to nurture, and her gifts to Ann now carry no hidden expectations. Ann can receive or refuse a gift without guilt. Dorothy can give money to Ann or not give money to her, because she no longer has to feel that she is buying Ann's time. The result is a happier relationship with improved communication.

True giving is unconditional. If it feels good to both giver and receiver, the gift carries no hidden hooks.

9. EVERYONE IS EQUAL AND HAS EQUAL OPPORTUNITIES IN LIFE (FALSE). The essence of each human being is equally precious. The universe needs each and every person to make the greater whole complete. However, each person is different. You do not have the same genes, early environment, life experiences, or level of awareness as anyone else. Therefore, it would be impossible to have any two people equal. This has been interpreted as negative by some; however, it is simply a fact of life. You make life easier for yourself when you know and accept your capabilities, talents, strengths, weaknesses, and potentials. You also make life easier when you make wise and realistic choices and put yourself in situations that are fair and advantageous for you.

For example, let us look at Jan, who works for a major hotel and was promoted recently to a management position. It did not take her long to realize how stressful this position was for her. Her basic personality traits require a sense of outside direction which includes clear, defined tasks. She likes an ordered, structured day and does not enjoy constant communication and confrontation. Jan was lucky that she knew herself well enough to create her old job back. She is happy not climbing the ladder of success and enjoys her structured, non-competitive job.

Look at your life and see if there are some areas that do not feel good that are putting you under stress. You may be acting under the false impression that every opportunity is good for you and that you should take all of them. On the other hand, if your life feels good and you do not wish to accept an opportunity to do something else, consider staying where you are as an acceptable choice.

Jenny, for instance, has never been happier than when she stays with her new baby and three-year-old. She has to choose either to return to her full-time job at the university where she has tenure or to stay at home with her children. She used to think she had the same needs as her peers (most of whom are men) and that she would be fulfilled by a prestigious career. Now she is finding that nurturing needs are more important for her to express at this time. She can re-create the job if that becomes important again (that is, if she has a guiding belief that says she can).

10. A DIFFICULT CHILDHOOD CRIPPLES YOU FOR LIFE (FALSE). Unwise parents and a negative childhood may cripple your life for a time; however, blaming parents who were themselves the products of a painful childhood helps no one. You can break out of early negative patterns; you do not have to remain handicapped forever. Limitations force us to grow. Our goal in life is wisdom, and we gain it by combining experience and knowledge. Knowing this does not take away our pain, but it helps us to deal intelligently with the process.

One simplified way of looking at your life is to see it in three stages. The *first stage* involves your parents and your life experiences from birth to around age 18. The circumstances of these years set up a matrix of patterns which you will work out in stage two. Self-awareness and wisdom are acquired in *stage two;* in this stage you heal your conflicts and solve your problems. Some of you are experiencing issues of conflict that have been handed down from generation to generation in areas such as parenting, self-esteem, religion, alcoholism, chronic depres-

TRUE AND FALSE GUIDING BELIEFS

Things You Were Taught That Are <u>False</u>

1. You cannot get what you want in life.
2. Expectations insure you will get what you want.
3. Get your wants met before your needs.
4. You are a victim.
5. You have to go to church to know God.
6. You will feel good when you have the "right" job, mate, car, etc.
7. Mistakes are bad.
8. It is better to give than to receive.
9. Everyone is equal and has equal opportunities.
10. Difficult childhoods always cripple you for life.

sion, communication in relationships, love, etc. Many people never move beyond stage two; they simply pass their patterns on to their children. This book is designed to help you work through stage two of your life. *Stage three* is reached when you truly know, love, and accept yourself as you are. Difficult early experiences need not prevent you from reaching stage three in your life. When you look at making peace with your childhood and resolving your conflicts, you see your parents and your early experiences as opportunities for growth.

One way to overcome the impact of early trauma is to go back over the memories in your mind, in as much detail as possible. You do this as an adult, having more mature insights into what was really going on. In this way you re-program your past and, thus, change its influence.

It is helpful to continue looking at your guiding beliefs to uncover those that no longer serve you. You will begin the process of being autonomous and being in charge of your own life. You will begin to free yourself from other people's belief systems that prevent you from being who you are capable of being—uniquely yourself. And this feels good.

Chapter Five

Tools for Change

> You are never given a wish without also being given the power to make it true. You may have to work for it, however.
>
> —Richard Bach, *Illusions*

Awareness is the first step in the process of change; many times you cannot change your behavior and guiding beliefs with your conscious mind alone. It is necessary to reprogram your subconscious mind as well. Whatever you do not like in your life, you can use your creative powers to re-create. Two techniques that can be useful in helping you to replace the actions, beliefs, attitudes and emotions that no longer serve you are affirmations and visualizations. In order to explain how these techniques work, it is important first to see how you create your experience of life. Then you can use these two techniques to create consciously and wisely whatever you want in your life.

Did you know that at some level of awareness you have created what is happening to you today? If some life situations seem to be beyond your control, at least consider that you do create your interpretation of these situations. You can choose to shut down and feel pain, boredom, restriction and unhappiness; or you can use everything to grow in consciousness. If you do not like what you are experiencing or feeling in life, you can change these things by using affirmations and visualizations as your tools.

Affirmations are positive statements that are healthy for you to say and hear in your mind. They can reshape the early guiding beliefs that conditioned you. You have dialogues called tapes or self-talk that run through your mind all the time and comment on your experiences. Such tapes are developed during your early years, and many of you hear as much as 90 per cent negativity. Some of your guiding beliefs are now unconscious to you. If you have not tried to list them, stop reading and do so now! You will see what is going on in your mind that no longer serves you. Changing negative mental dialogues to positive ones is instrumental to building self-esteem and to feeling good.

Your negative guiding beliefs can be turned into positive statements. I recommend that you list these in a journal. A journal is a book or notebook in which you write all of your new ideas and list your needs, wants, dreams, etc. Journals are discussed more fully in Section Two of this book.

Many people have a basic guiding belief prevalent in their families that says, "I am unworthy." You can take this guiding belief and turn it into an affirmation by wording it, "I care about myself. I accept myself, regardless of what other people think or feel about me." Or your affirming statement may be, "I accept myself the way I am," or "I feel loving toward myself." To make a personal affirmation from the negative self-talk that is now in your mind, simply turn the negative statement around and say its opposite. When you hear yourself, for example, saying in your mind, "Life is hard," simply reverse the statement and affirm, "Life is getting easier and easier every day."

I used to feel unworthy when I wanted to confront my husband to renegotiate some of the traditional roles we had set up in our early marriage. One example that comes to mind is my complaint that I was tired of doing boring, repetitive housework. I would ask for more participation on his part. The logical answer I received kept me stuck for a long time because I felt undeserving of help or of a change.

Rodney would say such things as, "I work long hours and, therefore, do not have the time or energy to participate." Or he would say, "I contribute more than you do around here—I build furniture, remodel the house, fix everything that is broken."

It took me quite a process to feel worthy, to feel strong enough to break out of this pattern. My thinking needed to be changed before I could solve the problem, confront, or feel deserving of a change. I got in touch with the guiding beliefs that tied me to this pattern:

"I am unworthy and do not have the right to get what I think is fair and right in this relationship."

"Good and giving people do not complain."

"A good wife is responsible and takes care of everything that is not handled by her husband."

"Disagreeing and confronting are bad, and a sign of an unhappy marriage."

When I became aware of a negative belief which had been guiding me to unwholesome behavior, I would create a countering affirmative statement which I used as an affirmation to restore my own balance. For example, I would say to myself:

"In a good relationship, people do not feel victimized."

"A good relationship has conflict."

"I deserve to express my needs and wants."

"I can have a maid if Rodney does not want to help."

After a time I would have converted myself over to the new belief system; but to complete the process, I would have to deal with the new beliefs objectively, also. I had to bring it up, confront and express it to Rodney (or to whoever might be involved in a given problem). We can only create in our lives what we believe we deserve, are capable of, and are willing to work for sufficiently to actually express our new creation. Until we get to that point, we can work through affirmations and other techniques on old, unhealthy beliefs that are keeping us stuck.

Eventually we grow from guidance by the subconscious (past conditioning) to consciousness. The conscious mind has the power to create new conditions by selecting new guiding thoughts, once we become aware of what is not useful or helpful in our prior conditioning. The subconscious mind is like a computer, operating only on the programs (beliefs, interpretations, attitudes) that have been put into it. As we become more and more conscious, we put better programming into our computer, and this empowers us to create our lives better.

The fastest way to use affirmations to reprogram your subconscious mind is to put them on a cassette tape and listen to them daily. It is helpful to close your eyes and use a light hypnosis or deep relaxation exercise before playing the tape. (Such exercises are included in Section Two under Affirmations.) This puts you in the alpha state of brain wave consciousness; you are most receptive to new ideas in this state. If you play your tape while driving, doing yard work, or housework, do not use the deep relaxation exercise because you need to be fully alert at those times.

Verbally repeat the affirmations you hear on your tape. Do this daily for at least three weeks. Depending on the degree of negativity experienced toward the new ideas, some people need to listen to the tape and verbalize their affirmations for much longer periods than others. It is good to continue the practice even after you start feeling better about yourself. Only you, listening to your inner needs, can determine how long to use your affirmations.

The purpose of your affirmations is to change the negative self-talk which has guided the belief system upon which you have lived up to now. In order to feel better about yourself, your beliefs about yourself that are untrue and are holding you back must change. Eventually you will be able to go through your life experiences with an automatic self-correcting thought pattern.

Let me share an example from my life. A few years ago I began my public speaking career by talking in front of my children's PTA. My topic was "Building Children's Self Esteem." I was so afraid of not looking like an expert and not doing a perfect job that I heard things in my mind such as, "Who do you think you are to stand up and tell people what they need to do?" and "If they disagree or challenge you, you'll look foolish."

The part of me that wanted to move ahead on the path of self-growth worked hard at cancelling these thoughts and creating the opposite ones. I repeated to myself, "You do have something to offer. Most people like to hear information that solves some of their problems. So what if someone disagrees with you? This information works for you." With this positive emphasis, I gave the talk and was very pleased.

Here are some tips on creating personal affirmations:

1. State simply what you are creating or asking for.

2. Avoid double negative statements and the word "not." Instead of saying, "I will not overeat today," say, "I will eat only when hungry today."

3. Avoid statements that you see as impossible. You can jump too far ahead of yourself in this process. Instead of saying, "I create a perfect relationship right now," say, "I am opening my mind to accept a perfect relationship."

Self Esteem is a place of

*Knowing Yourself

*Accepting Yourself

*Loving Yourself

*Enjoying Yourself

and

*Being Yourself

Affirmations have more power when combined with the techniques of creative visualization. Creative visualization is creating in your mind with your imagination what you want. Do not underestimate this power. With the thought you see or sense in your mind, you create tomorrow. As Flip Wilson's famous character Geraldine says, "What you see is what you get!" By creating new images of yourself, you begin moving in a new direction.

Let us look at Virginia and Danny, a married couple. They have reciprocal dramas or life scripts, and as a couple they match up very well to irritate one another into growing into a more conscious state of awareness. Virginia went into the relationship with very little to say. She was willing to give her power to make decisions to Danny; she felt that he was smarter and superior to her. Her feelings of low self-esteem matched up with Danny's. He had much to say. He was very opinionated and domineering, and he easily took over the decision-making role. He felt good about himself when Virginia was in an inferior position.

If Virginia wants to change her feelings of unworthiness, she can use creative visualization as a tool for growth. First she must realize that she holds back expressing herself because she feels inferior to her husband. Then she can decide to visualize and affirm herself as a deserving person in the relationship who is equal in value to her husband. A helpful practice for her might be to close her eyes and picture herself and Danny sitting face to face. She can then begin to affirm such things as, "I freely express my thoughts and feelings," and "I say what I think, feel and believe." And finally she can visualize the comfort and relief this view of herself allows her to feel.

She can picture Danny warm and smiling in this scene; she can also picture the scene with him frowning and disagreeing. Whatever his reaction, her visualization and affirmation of her own worthiness will remain constant. She can picture them getting past Danny's resistance and visualize peaceful and warm feelings inside herself. The more details Virginia can see, hear, and feel in her mental pictures, the more likely it is that her visualizations will be manifested in real experience. If Virginia tries to express her feelings to Danny without the use of visualization techniques, she may stop the moment he emotionally or physically pulls away from her and rejects her unfamiliar behavior. The visualization exercise prepares her to handle such rejection because she has already acted out the possibilities in her mind many times; she is prepared to express her feelings even if Danny becomes uncomfortable.

A visualization that would help Danny would be for him to see himself as a powerful and confident person even when Virginia disagrees with him. He can add power to the picture by also mentally affirming such things as, "I do not have to make Virginia wrong to feel good about myself," and "Feelings and opinions are not right or wrong," and "I accept Virginia's feelings and opinions. It is okay for Virginia to be an equal partner with me."

Often I run into people who do not like their lives and yet do not know what they want to create. If this is how you are feeling, I recommend that you find people whom you like or admire and emulate their behavior. Using people as role models gives you a place to start.

Sometimes it is easier to start by seeing the negative self-talk in someone else. You've heard a person who had just dropped something say, "I'm such a klutz!" Or, a person who forgets to record a check in the checkbook may say, "I'm not responsible with money. I just hate to work with numbers."

One person I used as a role model was Ken Keyes. When I first read one of his books, I was really amazed that he began his book with permission to use the material freely. I had never run into the idea of encouraging readers to circulate information from a book without getting formal permission from the author. I like that idea, and I feel inspired to do the same thing with this book.

You have my permission to quote freely from this book. I ask that you use the quotes for teaching purposes and limit them to 500 words or less.

You can use role models whom you have never met such as people from Hollywood or TV or from a book. Or you can model people you know who have a particular area in their life worked out the way that you would like yours to be. It could be that you like their marriage, their parenting style, or their way of handling their career, to name just a few. Role models that you choose can be very effective teachers if you visualize and affirm yourself doing similar things. Bill Cosby comes to mind when I think of a positive male figure for some people to use as a role model.

The purpose of affirmations and creative visualizations is to consciously create what you want to experience in your life. If this is a new idea for you, then realize that you have been creating your level of self-esteem (and with it your life experiences) unconsciously. You have merely been repeating what was taught to you in childhood and have accepted that as your whole life's script. You can change that inner programming and change the life experiences it brings you by the use of affirmations and visualizations. You can create what you want to experience, feel, and think, beginning now.

Chapter Six

The Author's Process of Writing This Book

"The journey is the destination."
—Marilyn Ferguson, *The Aquarian Conspiracy*

Many times people have asked me, "What is it like when you finally feel good about yourself and have sound self-esteem? And what is the process like to achieve that?"

I will share with you my process of writing this book. Living with sound self-esteem reminds me of the story of a young man who had sought enlightenment for a long time. He finally met a reknowned guru or wise person near the top of a mountain, and rushing over to the sage, he begged, "Please tell me what it is like after enlightenment!" To this the great guru replied, "Before enlightenment you chop wood and carry water; and after enlightenment you chop wood and carry water."

My answer could be no better than that of the wise guru to the young man. I still go through the processes of living day to day. I deal with frustrations, fears, challenges, rewards, and joys. The difference is that I now feel open and trusting and willing to experience whatever may come my way. Experience has shown that the more I can let go and flow with what comes along, the better I feel and the easier life seems.

If I were to describe myself right now, this is what I would say: I feel good and the most loving and accepting of myself that I have ever felt. I feel like I am on a mountain top, aware that there are many more mountains to climb, content to enjoy this one for awhile. I am so proud of myself for making the climb and acknowledge my strong will and desire to get here.

What's up here? To begin with, there is a person who is at home in her body on this planet earth. She respects the physical laws and is no longer fighting them or resisting them. I am comfortable here.

There is an excitement and anticipation of what the next moment will bring. I have a great desire to reach great numbers of people with the truth about themselves—that each is good and is a part of the Source. Until multitudes are available for my teaching, I appreciate the people in my life I am able to serve. I feel honored to have a life purpose which allows me to intimately know others and be part of their spiritual awakening.

I feel good and bright and sunny and accepting, as I did as a very young child. I am happy I cracked the code of who I really am and why I am here. I feel so grateful. I'm ready for what is next on my path of life. Fear is a feeling I no longer allow to stop me from growing and taking risks. I know that I am Love and I allow it to be me and flow through me. I am truly grateful for the family I am part of—my husband and children.

My perspectives have been developed in recent years by writing. I should mention that I have not always been a writer; I began writing as a technique for dealing with the great changes in my life in my thirties. Several times as I was gathering my thoughts to set them down in this book, I experienced deep insights which seemed to have application much broader than the personal incidents which precipitated them for me. Sharing my life success with others in person and in writing has been rewarding

THE AUTHOR'S PROCESS OF WRITING THIS BOOK

Feeling good is feeling worthy.

to me because it often helped them to take risks, and to believe more strongly that this information can change their lives as it has mine. For this reason, I would like to share with my readers my process of writing this book.

It began with a telephone call in early 1985 asking me to write an article on the class I teach called "Building Sound Self-Esteem." I agreed, and my first step was to clarify my own ideas, which bore strong resemblance to those of L. S. Barksdale. This was not surprising, since in my own growth process I had drawn heavily on his book, *Building Self-Esteem*. In fact, in writing my article, I saw myself summarizing in simple language his detailed program.

I felt good about the article, and I began using it to introduce new clients to the concepts. It enabled me to teach the information better because it provided a certain cohesiveness to groups which began with everyone reading my article. It helped to open useful channels of communication right from the start.

About six months after writing the article, I began a class with a guided meditation from John Price's *The Planetary Commission*. We were to imagine and fantasize the most exciting future possible. We were to let go of all limitations such as time, money, past performance, logic, and so forth, letting ourselves get totally into our fantasies.

In my own fantasy, I imagined myself in my later years, writing a book. I could see the book being a catalyst that helped me to teach on a much broader scale. I allowed myself to feel a yearning I had always kept hidden from myself: that of really wanting to be an influence in changing the consciousness of the planet. I wanted to teach people how to love, first themselves and then others, in an all-inclusive way. I pictured myself lighting candles of consciousness around the world, helping to further world peace. The book, in this mental picture, was central to that vision.

Not long afterward, writing my ideas down became a conscious, immediate need. It became not a project for

THE AUTHOR'S PROCESS OF WRITING THIS BOOK

the year 2020, but a necessity in 1985. So I started. The first step was to expand my article adding insights that would be helpful, organizing the details, and polishing the writing. It grew into a booklet.

Then I found myself blocked and had to put the work aside for a time during this period. Old fears and negative self-talk resurfaced. I feared that I had been overly bold or optimistic to think I could write a book. After all, hadn't I gotten a D in freshman English? (I forgot about getting an A when it was repeated.) And the first time I took a graduate course, didn't I drop out because I couldn't write the paper?

My constant interaction with others, encouragement from good friends, plus a strong desire to become more conscious, carried me across that passage to an incredible breakthrough. One day in early March, sitting in my back yard in the sun, I began putting the book into form. When I would sit by myself and get into that quiet, meditative state, all I had to do was write down what I heard in my mind. The things I needed to write just began to clarify themselves. I could feel the balance between my rational mind and my intuitive mind (the part I was beginning to know and trust). I organized with one part and filled in spaces with the other. It was like a state of total connection with myself, humanity, and God. The book seemed to have a life of its own, with me serving as an instrument through which it was written.

An incident which illustrates this attunement was getting the title for the book. People would say to me over and over that "Building Sound Self-Esteem" is too dull a title. I agreed. Many times I wrote down possible titles on a piece of paper, looking for a more suitable one, but none of them ever seemed right. Then one day I said strongly to myself, "This is doing it the hard way. Just give me the title!" Holding that thought firmly in mind, I went for a walk, and half way around the block I heard, "You Could Feel Good." I smiled and jumped up and down a couple of times as I said, "Thank you," and hurried home—the title was *exactly* right!

The next stage was not so easy, and not so much fun. It required clarifying my vision so others could see it and could receive its intended benefit. I am good at seeing the forest but not so good at seeing the trees. Interestingly, just at this point, many people came along to help me in dealing with the detail required to give birth to the book. My husband, for example, suggested that the last chapter of an early draft might be better as the first chapter. Other people showed up as needed to type parts of the book. During this period I found a typist in very good rapport with me. She and I kept refining the manuscript as many others continued to help edit and to give most excellent suggestions. Thankfully, I was not in an earlier life pattern of doing everything by myself; so I was able to accept this generous assistance. Much of it was freely offered, some of it I paid for in money, and some was paid for in counseling.

I have learned much about perfection through this writing. Primarily, I realize that there will never be a stopping place because a project like this will never be perfectly perfect. However, it has improved with every step, including the first "final copy" sent to the publisher—which he returned with encouraging comments but not with his acceptance.

I reworked the manuscript many times, especially when the publisher kindly offered his suggestions. The acorn symbol came to my mind each time I did so. I saw that the book, like the acorn, was perfect at each stage but it had to grow, through a long process, toward fuller stature.

Another part of my process involves how I was led to this particular publisher. Intellectually, I was aware that my book was written to help others. The information had helped me, and I had used it to help many others including family, friends, students, and clients. But actually publishing a book and spreading the information to multitudes seemed like a quantum leap. My attacks of uncertainty sounded very much like my earliest self-doubts: "Who's going to listen to you? Who do you

THE AUTHOR'S PROCESS OF WRITING THIS BOOK

think you are to tell people how to solve their problems? What if this information is not accepted outside your own network?"

I talked to friends who had published books. I learned how difficult it can be to find a publisher. I gathered the best advice I could from those who had succeeded, and even bought the *Writer's Market* as a practical step toward my goal.

Then it occurred to me to try my own intuitive processess—to use the techniques of visualization to help the book find a publisher. I pictured in my mind a pyramid of molecules. I imagined one molecule at the bottom, moving easily around and among other densely packed molecules; then moving unobstructed to the apex of the pyramid. I often visualized this successful molecule.

My faith was enhanced when I acted on my feelings and wrote a letter to the publisher I felt was right for my book. I had just finished reading Ken Carey's *Vision,* a book which left me feeling joyful and inspired. While reading it, I had felt my purpose was aligned with what Carey was presenting, so I sent a handwritten note to the publisher sharing this fact. I told him that I was writing a book on self-esteem and inquired about his possible interest in it. (Later I learned that what I wrote is known as a query letter and the usual protocol is to type it in a formal style and to expect a rejection letter in return). What I received instead was a hand-written note from Jim Gross, encouraging me to send him the manuscript.

I did so, and after reviewing it, he wrote that he would publish my book if I could put more of myself into it. I wrote the manuscript again, including more of my experiences and views, and sent him the second version. His reply was not prompt in coming, and old anxieties resurfaced as I watched and hoped for a letter of acceptance. When I did receive word, it was still not acceptance; yet I was grateful for his continued interest and for the generosity shown by this publisher in making still further suggestions to help a new author.

Determinedly, I wrote version three. This was a special discipline for me because I am not a detail person, and I had never before put forth such an effort to polish my writing or to tailor it to someone else's requirements.

Again, I had no word on the manuscript for a couple of months. I had asked for feedback, and waiting was difficult; but then I realized that the universe was providing feedback through two people other than the publisher. First, I reconnected with an old friend who kindly read the manuscript and made a good suggestion: she thought that summary charts at the end of each chapter would be helpful to readers, and she even styled and typed them for me on her computer.

Another especially helpful comment was from one of my students who said, "Your teaching style is different from your writing style. You teach in first person and write in third person." Her observation triggered my intuition to write this as the final chapter, where I am attempting to share myself with you in a way similar to the way I do with my clients and groups, face to face.

I could tell you of many other interesting experiences I have had in teaching, or tell you in detail about other insights I gained while writing this book; but you have the idea now that once you get into the process of Feeling Good, your growing as a person never stops. I am proof of that: I am learning and growing at this time in my life in more exciting ways than ever.

Writing this book has been a real adventure. It not only fulfills my desire to communicate these ideas more widely, it has also helped in further developing my classroom approach and has forced me to grow as a person. I believe my readers, in pursuing their own self-development, will also find in these ideas a catalyst essential to growth.

Remember to appreciate the processes of your life as much as your goals. This understanding applies to all of life's lessons. It has been life's processes that taught me to let go of control, to heal my fear of failure, to let

THE AUTHOR'S PROCESS OF WRITING THIS BOOK

others help me... and to connect in joyful encounter with my higher Self, which I know to be a part of the Source of all creativity.

Part II

Workbook for Feeling Good

Section One

The Self-Esteem Indicator

Your self-esteem indicator rating is important only to you, and is not to be compared with anyone else's. Save it and date your answers and your scores. Notice your high and low answers, but do not evaluate your worthiness based on your scores. Answer the questions again in about six months, and again date your answer page and your scoring. Your low answers help you to become aware of beliefs and patterns that block you from feeling good. These answers show where you can help yourself by creating personal affirmations or by using other appropriate exercises from this workbook. You will see growth and improvement as you work on difficult areas, but you need not judge the speed of your progress. You can grow and expand your awareness at your own rate.

If many of your answers are low, you will notice quick improvement by working with this book because you have many areas to work on. All the parts of you are interdependent, and a gain in one area strengthens your entire self. It is helpful to take the self-esteem indicator periodically, both to notice your areas of particular growth and to learn where you still need to work.

This self-esteem indicator is adapted from L. S. Barksdale's Self-Esteem Index No. 69. I greatly appreciate Barksdale for his pioneering work in this field. Building upon his foundation, I have been able to refine, innovate, and successfully apply his stated principles. If you wish to return to this source of my material, the address of the L. S. Barksdale Foundation is listed with other suggested readings on page 105.

THE HARRILL SELF-ESTEEM INDICATOR

This is a tool you may use to become more aware of and evaluate your degree of self-esteem. It is not a test with right or wrong answers. Remember! You *can* feel better about yourself.

Answer the questions reflecting how you currently feel and behave. Rate yourself on a scale of 0 to 4.

    0 = I almost NEVER feel or behave that way.
    1 = I RARELY feel or behave that way (25% of the time).
    2 = I SOMETIMES feel or behave that way (50% of the time).
    3 = I USUALLY feel or behave that way (75% of the time).
    4 = I almost ALWAYS feel or behave that way (100% of the time).

SCORE ... SELF-ESTEEM STATEMENTS

_____ 1. I accept myself the way I am right now.
_____ 2. I am worthy, simply because I exist. I do not have to earn my worthiness.
_____ 3. I get my needs met before I meet the needs of others.
_____ 4. I do not let it get me down when other people blame or criticize me.

THE SELF-ESTEEM INDICATOR

_____ 5. I do not allow others to hurt me or put me down.
_____ 6. I do not compare myself to other people.
_____ 7. I feel equal to other people regardless of my performance, looks, I.Q., or achievements (or lack of).
_____ 8. I take responsibility for my feelings and emotions. I do not blame others when I am upset, angry, or hurt.
_____ 9. I learn from my mistakes rather than use them to confirm my unworthiness.
_____ 10. I separate my behavior from the essence of who I am.
_____ 11. I understand that I can choose to love each human being without having an active relationship with them.
_____ 12. I accept other people as they are, even when they do not meet my expectations or I dislike their behavior.
_____ 13. I am not responsible for anyone else's actions, needs, thoughts, moods, or feelings; only for my own.
_____ 14. I feel my own feelings and think my own thoughts, even when those around me think or feel differently.
_____ 15. I am kind to myself and do not use "shoulds" and "oughts" to put myself down with value judging.
_____ 16. I allow others to have their own interpretation and experience of me.
_____ 17. I look for something positive in each individual I meet.
_____ 18. I forgive myself and others for making mistakes and being unaware.
_____ 19. I accept responsibility for my interpretation of other people's behavior and my responses to them.
_____ 20. I do not dominate others or allow others to dominate me.

_____ 21. I am my own authority. I make decisions that are for others' good and my own highest good.
_____ 22. I develop and use my talents.
_____ 23. I balance giving and receiving in my life.
_____ 24. I am responsible for changing what I do not like in my life.
_____ 25. I choose to love and respect every human being including myself.

Add up your score. It is a percentile giving you feedback on your degree of self-esteem (love of self). Place no judgments as to what is a good score. Use the questions where you assigned a lower number as an indication of where you might benefit from change. Create affirmations (using positive language) and visualizations of how you want things to be to improve how you feel.

Section Two

Affirmations

Creating Your Own Personal Affirmations

1. Listen to your mind talk.

2. List in your journal your negative thoughts, attitudes, and guiding beliefs.

3. Turn them around and affirm the opposite. Example: When I am tied up in traffic and am going to be late for an appointment, I may say in my mind, "You idiot, you didn't allow enough time. Why are you always so late?"
I can create these affirmations:
    - I am learning to be a punctual person by paying attention to time.
    - I am learning what prevents me from being on time.
    - I am in the process of allowing extra time for unexpected delays.
    - I give myself permission to be late.
      -or-
    - I am late this time and have to accept this. I will make a point of paying attention to time, in the future.

Making Your Own Affirmation Tape

It is helpful to reprogram your unhealthy guiding beliefs by listening to a cassette tape with statements that you now want to direct your life. The Barksdale book, which you can order from the Barksdale Foundation, has 50 such affirmations. You can also make up your own or use some of the relevant ones which I have included in this book. It is very powerful to use your own voice in making this tape.

Here is how to make a tape:

1. If the tape is for meditation and you can relax in a quiet place, put a relaxation exercise at the beginning. If you are driving in a car, do not listen to the relaxation exercise on your tape.
2. Read your affirmation three times; leave a pause after each reading to allow yourself time to affirm the statement to yourself mentally.
3. End the tape by counting from one to five and giving yourself the suggestion that you are fully alert on the count of five.
4. A good tip for making any relaxation tape: talk slowly and use very little inflection in your voice, as if you were a monotone.

If you are using the tape to relax in a quiet place, here is a relaxation exercise; you can include your own affirmations at the appropriate place in the exercise.

1. *Relaxation Exercise*

Sit or lie down with your eyes closed, your arms and legs uncrossed, spine straight, and hands resting in your lap. Imagine yourself in your favorite place. See it, sense it, feel it. Focus on your breath and breathe in slowly to the count of four and breathe out slowly to the count of four. Do this several times. Then say to yourself, "I am peaceful and relaxed." If you begin to feel tense or unable to relax during this exercise, focus again on your breath. Imagine a light resting on the top of your head. It is a bright, radiant, comfortable light. Imagine that this light has the power to relax any tight places in the muscles of your body. Now, allow this light to come into your head and slowly flow down through your whole body. As the light finds a tense place in your body, it stops and radiates warmth and kindness to this place, and the tension releases. The light continues until your whole body is peaceful and relaxed.

2. *Affirmations*

Read your affirmations slowly three times; leave a pause after each reading to allow yourself time to affirm the statement to yourself mentally. Imagine that each statement is already true. Use all your senses to experience each statement. Imagine yourself seeing or sensing yourself in this new level of awareness where the affirmation is already in operation in your life.

3. *Ending the Tape*

It is now time to bring your consciousness back to this room. Begin moving and stretching your muscles. You feel refreshed and rested, as if you have had a couple of hours of sleep. Open your eyes on the count of five. One, two, three, four, five. Your eyes are now open.

Affirmations

Love

I am worthy simply because I exist.
I unconditionally accept myself right now, this moment.
I let go of all the reasons that keep me from un-conditionally loving myself and others.
I fulfill my needs so I can give to others.

Growth

Everything that comes my way is an opportunity for my growth even if it feels bad.
I feed myself physically, emotionally, mentally, and spiritually in order to grow in a positive way.
I am perfect at each stage of my development.
I accept my life challenges as opportunities for my growth.

Communication

I am learning to be genuine in all my relationships.
I listen as well as talk to myself.
I balance my listening and talking with others.
I am open and honest with myself and others.

Control

I allow others and myself the opportunity to say, think, feel, and do whatever we choose without judgment.
I release my past patterns from controlling me.
I am learning to respond with wisdom rather than react to people and events.
I let go and flow into this moment.

AFFIRMATIONS

Planning

I ask today for what I need and let things flow to me as fast as I can handle them.
I ask for what I need and want, and I trust the journey of life to take me there.
I balance my plans with the needs of others.
I let go of how and when my needs and desires are fulfilled.

Parenting

I encourage my children to think, act, and say what they need to do to reach their potential.
I give my children feedback from the heart and not criticism from the head.
I balance my needs with my children's needs.
I allow my children to gradually separate from me as they grow up.

Divorce

I wish my former spouse well.
I let go of what other people think and expect of me.
I accept what is best for me and my partner.
I let go of my partner when she/he needs to leave.

Will and Power

I align my will with the greater good.
I allow right action to flow through me.
I let go of controlling myself and others and accept what is and what needs to be.
I use my power wisely.

Prosperity

I accept opulence in my life.
I deserve to create what I need and want.
I accept money as an exchange for my services and talents.
I balance all my debts to others and release what I think others owe me.

Authority

I am my own authority.
I accept the choices I make and accept their consequences.
I release situations where I dominate another or am dominated.
I am responsible for my thoughts, words, and actions, and I accept the consequences.

Anger

I let go of feeling like a victim.
I release unreal expectations.
I am not the cause of other people's anger.
I express my anger by talking, writing, or exercising.

Weight

Everything I think, feel, and do takes me to my perfect weight.
Every day in every way I release the blocks to reaching my perfect weight.
I allow my body to move toward my perfect weight.
I desire to weigh _____ lbs.

AFFIRMATIONS

Body

I listen to my body.
I open myself to giving my body what it needs.
I enjoy living in this physical form.
I take care of my body today.

Relationships

I release unreal expectations of my partner.
I accept the life lessons that come my way through my relationship with _____.
I consciously choose this relationship with _____ to share life's journey.
My partner mirrors aspects I need to see in myself.

Jealousy

No one can take what is mine.
There is enough love for all of us.
I let go of wanting to control my partner.
My security needs are met, and I let go of jealousy.

Envy

I no longer compete with others; I do what is right for me.
There is enough for both of us to win.
I am happy _____ (name) has achieved _____ (name the achievement).
I win when others win.

Here and Now

I am right here now, and this is the right place for me now.

YOU COULD FEEL GOOD

I plan for the future, learn from the past, and focus my attention on now.
Right now I am experiencing exactly what I am thinking and feeling.
I am living this moment, right here, right now, for my highest good.

Section Three

Visualizations

Visualizations are pictures that you see in your mind. Some people see clear visual pictures when they close their eyes, and some do not. Some people are inclined to be more auditory (sense through hearing), and others are more kinesthetic (sense in terms of feeling). Those of you who are not visual can still visualize by closing your eyes and sensing what you are creating in your mind. Practice a minute. Close your eyes and sense the difference between your car and your neighbor's car. Your impression is visualization whether you see the cars clearly or not.

Consciously working with visualizations is similar to working with affirmations. You are creating your future by the conscious images you see in your mind. Why not become aware of them and have them create positive realities for you?

You can take each of the affirmations presented in this book and use them for visualizations. While you say one of the affirmations, close your eyes and imagine what it would look like and feel like if it were already true. This is a part of a lifestyle change. You make your affirmations more powerful by putting your mind behind your words in order to create what you want. You can use the visual technique to create anything you want to experience in your future. You can use it to break out of old patterns, to change how you relate to other people, to attract the joy or relationship you want, or to build self-esteem.

Create Your Own Visualizations

It is possible to create your own personal pictures. Do you catch yourself thinking and seeing yourself in a negative way? Turn those thoughts around just as you did in creating an affirmation. See a positive picture in your mind.

Example 1: Sandra reviews in her mind a mistake that she made today. She forgot to mail an important letter for her boss. She became defensive and angry at her boss when he made blaming remarks. In order to create a different response in herself, Sandra used creative visualization. She began changing her defensive, angry reaction by changing the picture in her mind so that she made the mistake without feeling bad about herself. She simply accepts responsibility for her mistake and is willing to pay the consequence of displeasing her boss. She visualizes the scenario again and changes her actions if she wants to. She sees herself actively communicating with her boss using "I" messages. "I see how important it was to you that I send the letter this morning, and I apologize." She sees her boss listening, nodding her head, and letting go of the need to blame Sandra. Such a visualization has a positive effect the next time Sandra's boss blames her for something.

Example 2: Dennis, a salesman, needs to be open and friendly when he calls on a client for the first time. He generally feels ill at ease around strangers, finds meeting new people difficult, and is shy until he knows someone. Dennis wants to keep this job and wants to actively change how he feels in the presence of others. In therapy he is learning what some of his early family patterns were that conditioned him and what his innate traits are. Visualization helps him get over his initial fear of meeting new people. He pictures a scene in his mind of an uncomfortable sales call and then repictures the scene with changes he wants to claim for himself. For one, he incorporates small talk in his picture of a first meeting with someone. Before using visualization techniques Dennis was too serious, and therefore he was anxious to conclude the interview. Dennis jumped too quickly to talking about business. His work with mental images has positively affected his job. Before calling on new clients now, Dennis rehearses in his mind the new qualities he has claimed for himself. Because Dennis uses visualization, he not only likes his job better and feels more confident, he has increased his sales, too.

Running through different possible outcomes gives you the mental training to handle a similar problem in the future in a new way. Remember, what you see is what you can create in the future.

Section Four

Summary: Thoughts to Ponder

1. You are okay even when your behavior is inappropriate.

2. You have control over your inner world—your thoughts, attitudes, perceptions—even if you do not like the events in your life or what others say, do, or think.

3. The clue that you judge yourself or others is the use of "should" and "ought" messages in what you say and think. For example, you "should" clean the house for company. It is important to do what you consciously want to do and be willing to live with your decisions. You may choose to clean, not because you "should" clean, but because you want to have an ordered appearance for company. Or you may choose not to clean the house, accept your inner feelings, and share it with them.

4. Compare yourself only to yourself in order to see where you are going and where you have been; never compare yourself to someone else for the purpose of putting one of you down.

5. You are doing your best at each moment -
   - Even if someone tells you differently

- Even if you "know" better.
- Even if you want to change and are unable to yet.
- Even if you once were able to do better.

6. Love yourself and others simply because we all exist. Let go of earning love and keeping a tally.

7. Change and growth is a process. We never arrive. There is always more to learn, develop, and experience in life.

8. Make note of your current needs so that you can get them met consciously and appropriately.

9. All behavior makes sense when you look at the needs behind the behavior.

10. You are a perfect expression of your Self right now, this instant. Take this view of yourself into the future.

11. Building sound self-esteem is a process of learning to love yourself unconditionally.

Section Five

Further Suggestions

1. Join a support, growth, or therapy group.

2. Take self-awareness classes.

3. Get counseling.

4. Read books on self-awareness and spiritual growth.

5. Keep a journal.
   - Write lists of your needs, wants, and desires.
   - Record your dreams.
   - Write what you want to experience in life.
   - List your blocks.
   - List your fears.
   - Write letters to anyone you are angry or unforgiving towards. You do not have to mail the letter.
   - Answer the questions titled "Getting to Know Myself" to get you started.
   - Write a poem of forgiveness to someone in your life.

Here is an example:

A Poem to Rodney
Suzanne Harrill
April, 1986

Rodney, I may have forgotten to thank you for being you.
Yes, there have been so many years where
All I wanted was for you to change and be different.
That is behind us now, because
I now know the Truth.
It was always I whom I wanted to be different,
And since it was too painful,
I projected my fears and self-destructive
Thoughts and feelings onto you.
Please forgive me for when I did not know:
Those years of ignorance and immaturity.
I turn now to the present and see a
Joyful, radiant being unfolding as you.
Thank you for being you and for touching my life.

Getting to Know Myself

Define, explain, and give examples:

1. Do you believe the universe is ordered or chaotic? Do things happen for a reason or by chance?

2. Do you believe man is basically good or evil? Why?

3. Do you believe in a higher power than yourself? Explain.

4. How do you explain evil? Who is responsible for it?

5. Why does "man" live? Why does "man" die?

FURTHER SUGGESTIONS

6. What is creativity? Who possesses it? Can it be learned?

7. Does consciousness evolve? Explain.

8. Who is in charge of your life?

9. Who judges your life? Is this fair?

10. Are you a complete entity on your own, or do you need another to be complete?

11. How do you explain natural disasters?

12. What are the differences between your needs and wants? List some of both.

13. List ten of your guiding beliefs.

14. When are you the most content?

15. What is the most negative feeling you have about yourself?

16. What are some of your greatest fears? How did you get them? Do they serve you?

17. How do you live with your fears?

18. What are your strengths? How do you know them? Have you proven them?

19. Who do you believe has hindered your growth? List examples and give times it has occurred in your life. Are you ready to release them and make peace with them?

20. What life circumstance do you find most painful? Most joyful?

21. What is your most developed side—mental, emotional, or physical? Your least? What things do you need to do to balance yourself?

22. Define your concept of God, or Source, or Universe.

23. Take an event from your past—one that still hurts or bothers you—and write a letter to the person or people involved. Do not give them the letter. Next, thank the person(s) who hurt you for the hidden gifts in the experience. What did you learn from the person or the experience?

24. Who has taught you the answers to the above questions? Do you want to explore any further answers and search for further meaning? What in particular?

25. Pretend you are writing a novel. As the author, you choose the parents, family, and early life circumstances in order to create a context for the main character, you. Take your story up to the present time and explain your rationale for having these experiences, people, and events show up for your character. Now look into the future and show how this character can use those early life experiences to the best advantage. Where could the early experiences be a catalyst or motivator to do or experience something down the road?
(Purpose: This exercise helps many people move beyond a difficult childhood, a traumatic event, or a difficult period in life.)

Section Six

Self-Awareness Exercises

1. Ask a question about a problem that you want insight into before you fall asleep.

2. Whenever you are confused, write down what the problem is and what you want or need as a solution.

3. Take a sheet of paper and fold it in half and then in half again. There are four quadrants when you open the paper. In the four quadrants, write several answers to the following questions:
   Quadrant 1: Who am I?
   Quadrant 2: What do I want in life that is not here now?
   Quadrant 3: What things block or keep me from what I want?
   Quadrant 4: What do I need to do in order to move past the blocks and create what I want in my life?

Example

1. I am

    curious
    nurturing
    growing
    a mother
    a wife
    a part of a greater whole
    creative

2. I want

    to travel
    to exercise
    to paint
    to know God
    to communicate
    to feel good about myself
    to be alone more

3. My blocks are

    money

    time

    the need to do what I think is expected of me
    fears about receiving

4. What I need to do is

    rearrange priorities on how I spend my money
    stop spending time where it does not serve me
    work on my self-esteem

    let go of what others think

Section Seven

Suggested Readings

Bach, Richard. *Illusions.* New York, NY: Dell Publishers, 1977.

Barksdale, Lilburn S. *Building Self-Esteem.* Idyllwild, CA: The Barksdale Foundation, 1972.

Bloomfield, Dr. Harold H. and Felder, Leonard. *Making Peace with Your Parents.* New York, NY: Random House, Inc., 1983.

Briggs, Dorothy. *Your Child's Self-Esteem.* New York, NY: Doubleday, 1970.

Dyer, Dr. Wayne W. *Pulling Your Own Strings.* New York, NY: Thomas C. Crowell Co., 1978.

Fields, Rick, et al. *Chop Wood, Carry Water.* Los Angeles, CA: Jeremy P. Tarcher, Inc., 1984.

Gawain, Shakti. *Creative Visualization.* Mill Valley, CA: Whatever Publishing, 1978.

Gray, John. *What You Feel You Can Heal.* Santa Monica, CA: Heart Publishing Co., 1984.

Jampolsky, Gerald G. *Love Is Letting Go of Fear.* Berkeley, CA: Celestial Arts, 1979.

Keyes, Ken. *Handbook to Higher Consciousness.* St. Mary, KY: Living Love Publications, 1972.

Peck, Scott M. *The Road Less Traveled.* New York, NY: Simon & Schuster, 1980.

Segal, Jeanne. *Living Beyond Fear.* North Hollywood, CA: Newcastle Publishing Co., Inc., 1984.

Appendix

Letters from Clients

I would like to introduce you to five people with whom I have worked. They will share with you here their experiences of how this information has affected their lives. I have included these letters to impress upon you that this information works not only for me but for other people as well—people like you.

Self Discovery

by K. L.

As a result of Suzanne Harrill's self-esteem class, I've overcome some old childhood fears and begun an exciting process of personal and spiritual growth.

I signed up for the class because I was very upset in my new job, which included secretarial duties at a new advertising agency. I agreed to perform these duties, among others, in return for a chance to write advertising copy with a good creative director. My previous professional experience included advertising and public relations management, media sales, and newspaper journalism.

Well, I hated the secretarial stuff. So much, in fact, that I cried almost every day in the bathroom. I figured this new job was threatening my sense of self-worth. And

I wanted to know why. I remembered reading about Suzanne's class on self-esteem, so I called her for a counseling session. She mentioned the phrase "fear of a female subordinate role" and I knew instantly that's what I had. I decided to take her self-esteem class with the goal of discovering why.

I found out that my aversion to any role where I didn't have control over my own schedule and might not be respected for my intellectual and creative abilities went back to my childhood. The challenge was to separate my sense of self-worth from my title, salary, office, and other status symbols to which I was accustomed, and I learned to do this in Suzanne's class. I do less secretarial work now. What I still do doesn't trigger emotional upset, though I don't like it any more than I did at the outset. The difference is that I possess greater self-esteem. I understand my worth as a person doesn't depend on my job.

I approach everything—family life, my job and professional commitments with more serenity and a sense I'll rise to meet whatever circumstance occurs in my life. My family and friends have noticed the difference, which has enriched their lives too. I communicate freely with the people I love. I'm beginning to acquire inner peace. I truly believe self-esteem, loving myself, is the first step toward the state of well-being I'm cultivating in my life.

With this new self-acceptance, I've also begun a rewarding process of self-discovery. I'm gaining a sense of my life's purposes. I'm also gaining a sense of how my past experience has prepared me for these purposes. This sense is like a religious feeling. I call it spiritual awareness and it enriches my life.

APPENDIX: FIVE PEOPLE SHARE THEIR EXPERIENCES

My Own Life

by J. S.

Before I learned that I am responsible for my own life, I was everyone's victim. Everything in my life happened because of causes beyond my control. I was constantly blaming others as well as the world around me for all circumstances in my life that I viewed as both fortunate and unfortunate. If I were late for work, the Houston traffic was to blame. If I didn't finish a work assignment, it was because I had too many interruptions or my work load was too heavy. If I ran out of gas, it was because I got stuck in traffic. For everything that happened in my life, there was a force that was bigger and more powerful than I was, and it was working against me at all times. I seemed to bounce from one disaster to another—always surviving to tell the tale and exhausted from the effort of just living from day to day.

When first confronted with the fact that I was responsible for my own life and well being, I was skeptical, angry, and curious. I did know that other people's lives seemed to work better than mine. I'd always considered it luck. This meant that it wasn't good fortune at all. They were actually doing something I wasn't doing, and because they were doing it, their life was working for them instead of against them. Little by little, I incorporated this idea into my life. It was not easy. To take full responsibility for my life meant that I couldn't blame anyone other than myself for whatever happened. It also meant that I would have to give up the high drama that had been a part of my life for so many years. I would no longer be a passive victim of life's misfortunes, but instead, I'd be an active participant. I could actually create what I wanted. If I wanted to suffer, I created situations in which I could suffer. If I did not want to suffer, I could take the same situation and look at it differently and not suffer.

As I experimented with being responsible for my own life and well being, life became easier and more enjoyable. Instead of struggling with life's problems, I was flowing with life's opportunities and experiences.

I was able not only to allow other people to be responsible for their own life and well-being but also to encourage them. I no longer felt responsible for them. I could support them by sharing and listening, and I could be free to let them handle whatever was happening in their lives as best they could. L. S. Barksdale in his book, *Building Self-Esteem*, states, "No one can possibly put himself in another's place as a valid point of reference, for no one else in the entire world has the same degree of awareness."

To me, this was frightening. It meant that everyone could do things his own way. I had to let go of the idea that I was always right and my ways were always right. They were only right for me.

Giving up being judgmental is not easy. I often will try to visualize myself in another person's circumstances and to understand how I would feel in their situation. Before, I would try to understand how they would feel. Since I had not lived the life they'd lived nor had the experiences they'd had, all I could do was judge what they'd done or how they'd reacted by my own experiences. If they did what I would have done, I thought they were right; and if they didn't, I thought they were wrong. Now I can let them be true to themselves without labeling rightness or wrongness. It's nothing more than their own way; it's what their experience of life has taught them.

I've discovered that I have more time to enjoy my life now that I understand that I am not responsible for everyone else in the world. I am responsible only for me. I am not responsible for teaching everyone else to live their lives as I live mine. L. S. Barksdale says it this way: "I am a unique and precious being, ever doing the best my current awareness permits." And so are you.

APPENDIX: FIVE PEOPLE SHARE THEIR EXPERIENCES

Suzanne Harrill—Counselor, Teacher, Friend

by M. J.

I moved to Houston four months ago. I was diagnosed as suffering from chronic depression, resulting from an emotional breakdown. I came to live with a relative.

Prior to meeting Suzanne, I had attempted suicide three times. I was so depressed I saw no hope. Every day, I thought of more gruesome ways to end my life.

Needless to say, I was in desperate need of therapy. I telephoned several therapists before calling Suzanne. Lack of sufficient monies was a problem for me. Consequently, there was no one to help. However I called Mrs. Suzanne Harrill and she agreed to counsel me. The fact that I was poor and had nothing to give her did not matter.

Upon meeting Suzanne, she gave me a hug. Suzanne had read an autobiography she had me write. We began to go over the information and I cried a lot and started releasing some of the hurt. Suzanne treats mental illness with love.

The next four sessions, Suzanne introduced me to metaphysics. I desperately needed something that would put me on my journey to "seeing the light." I was totally reclusive. I was dominated by fear. I could not bear to even go to the window and look out. I had been indoors for six months with the curtains drawn. I couldn't bear sunlight, and trusted no one.

Suzanne began telling me about the healing power of love, and that I would have to try and cooperate. I was reluctant because I had never heard of the things she was talking about. But I sure didn't have anything to lose. Suzanne began piling books based on love and forgiveness on me. I was still filled with fear of the outside world. So I continued to stay indoors and shut myself off.

I had the books Suzanne had given me. I began to read and read. Suzanne would discuss the material with me.

As I began to truly forgive those I thought had hurt me, I began to feel free. I went to the window and was able to look out without shaking and see not only with my physical eyes, but with my new spiritual ones, as well.

I can go outside now and I don't panic as I once did. I'm not well totally, but I've come a long way. My progress would not have been possible if Suzanne Harrill had not taught me the process of self-healing and building self-esteem. I'm learning to feel good.

APPENDIX: FIVE PEOPLE SHARE THEIR EXPERIENCES

I Accept Myself

by E. B.

I was taught that everyone was better than I. I think my mother used it, the comparison, to motivate. Daily there were screams and directives that I was no good, that others could do it better, and that I would rot in hell, and that perhaps she'd better boil Jane Doe's urine and make me drink it and maybe that would make me a good student, a good daughter, etc. These statements have haunted me most of my adult life. I really believed I was no good. I was full of hate and rage and envy. There were nightmares almost every night of people after me. Bloody, gory, horrible nightmares, filled with people who wanted to kill me, usually one at a time. They always had a weapon, a rifle or a knife. There was always a chase. There was always blood. There was always death at the end and I would always win. On the other hand, the nightmare left me so frightened, if I remembered it in the middle of the night, that I felt, now that I think about it, that I didn't really win. Daytime would erase any memory of the dream and there was rarely any fear if I did recall details.

In spite of the turmoil inside, outside I guess I passed muster. I have always had lots of friends and my job is somewhat satisfying, or so it would seem to many people. Deep down inside, and it started surfacing during the last three years, I wanted to die. I didn't want to commit suicide, I just wanted to die. I was so tired. When I started therapy, I didn't really have hope, but what the heck, I was alive so I guess I was looking for relief. I read all the suggested reading material and it helped.

I just couldn't convince myself that I was good, and I felt uncomfortable when people loved me, if I believed them. Usually I didn't believe them. I finally discovered that God had made me and therefore I had to be perfect. It was many, many months before I caught on. I'm still not always convinced that I'm okay. I have moments when I feel utter rejection if someone doesn't want to see me. And other times, I don't need another person's rejection to make me feel worthless. Those belief systems that my mother instilled in me drift back into mind at odd moments. I mustn't forget to mention that you, Suzanne, were the first person that I believed accepted me for what I was and loved me unconditionally. I had never heard of unconditional love. Maybe that's all it takes—one person to love a forsaken soul (body?) and to make that person see the light. I have a new life now. I almost love myself. The nightmares are gone. The rage is dissipating. The anger is dying. Envy is about the only negative emotion that dances around me, but I recognize it, I am ever conscious of the reason for its being, and I anxiously await its death. All this happened within a year's time. The best part is that I don't hate my mother any more. I guess that was part of the bargain: if I like myself, I'll like other people. It happened automatically. And the very best part was her sigh of relief when I told her I wasn't angry and more. That's also self-esteem: taking the burden of guilt off people who know they have hurt you, because they are probably hurting more than you.

APPENDIX: FIVE PEOPLE SHARE THEIR EXPERIENCES

Self-Esteem: When I Found It and What I Do With It

by N. E.

I remember well the day four years ago, when a friend invited me to attend a course on "Building Self-Esteem." My thoughts were, "I don't have any self-esteem; do I need it to attend a course?" "Will people know?" and "Do I want to attend a course on something I don't have, because I might end up with some and then what will I do with it?"

Having self-esteem meant to me that you liked yourself, you thought you were pretty wonderful, you had something to offer. I felt that I was void of self- esteem. I was not likable, or wonderful; nor did I have anything to offer. I'll admit that on occasion I would catch a glimpse of having what I thought was self-esteem. On occasions when I received a lot of praise from someone, when I really did something right, I would like myself, briefly. It did not take long to doubt that praise, and I learned to invalidate any praise coming from my family and friends. They were just doing that because they were close to me. They had to praise and support me whether they meant it or not.

Four years later (and ego aside, but never far away), I can admit to having sound self-esteem. Sometimes I feel high, sometimes low. Sometimes I curse myself and sometimes I love myself. Sometimes I run around with it looking for validation, and sometimes I try to coax others into taking my power from me so I can move back into that familiar sub-low self-esteem level that I once perfected.

Once that awareness kicked in and started feeding me constant reminders, I started doing things differently. I am aware that my self-esteem is my responsibility. I control the fluctuations in mood depending on how I feel about me in any given situation and I can control those fluctuations. At times I don't like me very much. At times I like me a lot. I still sometimes look for that validation from others to prove to me that I am worth something. I am aware, however, of my drama and I'm learning that validation of myself can come from my Self. I've learned that my behavior can be separated from my self-worth. If I'm mad at me for something that I have done, I can acknowledge that behavior and what I did not like about it and then I can be gentle with myself and realize that, difficult as it sometimes is to believe, I did the best that I could at that moment.

Learning about my own self-esteem has helped me to accept others as well as myself. When I'm not judging myself, I'm free to love others. I find that I attract people who do not have this information that I now have, and I have the opportunity to teach and reaffirm to myself. I want to teach my five-year- old son about self-esteem. It's so exciting when he picks up on something that I was not aware of until I was in my late twenties. I want to teach my mother, a very kind and self-sacrificing lady who takes care of everyone but herself. I want to teach my ex-husband, who was laid off from his job and regulates his self-worth accordingly. I want to teach a friend who has not yet learned to accept compliments and believes he deserves suffering more than he deserves happiness.

I do a lot of things differently now. I'm aware, and that awareness does not go away. I'm learning, against my will at times. I'm teaching what I need to learn. I acknowledge myself, usually in my journal, for things I have said and done and for things I have not said and have not done. I notice the self- esteem of others and try to understand why they are in the place they are in. I'm more open, definitely more assertive, and I share easily. Right now I'm acknowledging myself for having written this, and I'm beating myself up because it isn't perfect, and I accept both of those feelings and know that it is okay to be in both places at the same time, isn't it?

POEM BY A FRIEND

Little Acorns
Nanci Engle
March, 1986

Little Acorns never worry
When the winds begin to blow.
They go where gentle breezes lead them,
They grow where they need to grow.

Little Acorns know they're different
From all the others on the tree.
They don't try to force their future,
They know they're where they need to be.

Little Acorns never worry.
They have the strength of God within
To realize their own perfections
And learn from everywhere they've been.

So when you find yourself afraid of life,
Not liking who you've grown to be,
Please hold this image and remember
Little Acorns are like you and me.

This is a song a friend wrote for me.

Conclusion

A FINAL THOUGHT

I believe each of us is on a journey to discover who and what we are in the context of the greater whole, or the universe. It is as if we are weaving our own personal tapestry. Each life experience, book, teacher, and insight helps us advance on our journey. It is my wish to give you a few threads for your tapestry. Remember to love and accept where you are, as you are creating your tapestry, because life is a process without a final goal of arriving. There is always more from which to learn, grow, and experience.

Final affirmation: I FEEL GOOD!

*Namasté,

Suzanne

---

*"I honor the place in you where the entire universe resides, I honor the place in you of love, of light, of truth, of peace. I honor the place within you where if you are in that place in you and I am in that place in me, there is only one of us."

—Ram Dass, *Grist for the Mill*

Books and Products to help establish
The Global Spiritual Awakening

 Suzanne Harrill has shared deeply of herself in this book, and has presented fundamentally important concepts from a high perspective. She is working on another book that will have a lot more to say about that special perspective she has found. She also has created some self-esteem tapes which she has available, live tapes from some of her classes. See next page for ordering her tapes.
 Suzanne's efforts match our own—we at Uni★Sun are doing our best to publish books and offer products that make a real contribution to the global spiritual awakening that has already begun on this planet. For a free copy of our catalogue, please write to:

Uni★Sun
P. O. Box 25421
Kansas City, Missouri 64119
U.S.A.

CASSETTE TAPES
on
YOU COULD FEEL GOOD

Experience being in Suzanne's Building Self-Esteem class. This is a live class that has been edited. These three tapes reinforce the concepts taught in this book. To order, send $25.00 plus $3.00 for postage and handling to:

> Suzanne Harrill
> 2284 W. Holcombe #204
> Houston, Texas 77030

Texas residents add 8% sales tax. ($2.00)